PLAIN ANSWERS AND EXPLANATIONS ABOUT BEING A **CHRISTIAN** & SOME OTHER IMPORTANT CHURCHY STUFF

PLAIN ANSWERS AND EXPLANATIONS ABOUT BEING A **CHRISTIAN** & SOME OTHER IMPORTANT CHURCHY STUFF

SOME GOOD ANSWERS
TO SOME IMPORTANT QUESTIONS

DAVID SCOTT, ED.D., D.MIN.

PURPLE CHAIR BOOKS
AND EDUCATIONAL PRODUCTS, LLC.

PCB

Published by Purple Chair Books and Educational Products, LLC

First Printing, 2025

Copyright © David Scott, 2025

Scott, David 1969-

Plain Answers and Explanations About Being a Christian

By David Scott

ISBN: 978-1-953671-05-9

Subject: Christian Life/ Spiritual

Printed in the United States of America

Interior designed by Md Al Amin

Cover designed by Md Al Amin

ACKNOWLEDGMENTS

I want to express my gratitude to all the men and women of God who are my fellow "yoke men" in the Gospel. Your encouragement and motivation have inspired me to strive for excellence and spiritual perfection.

DEDICATION

This book is dedicated to all who have inspired and supported me along my journey. Your prayers, insights, and challenges have been instrumental in completing this vital work. Thank you for your love, faith, support, and continuous encouragement. Each of you is a valued and cherished part of my life.

TABLE OF CONTENTS

INTRODUCTION

Never have so many people desired God's word's simplicity, power, and truth. In this critical time for humanity, as God adds to the Church (the body of Christ), there is a need for clear, direct, and sound answers to specific questions about the Christian life. Providing practical, straightforward, and biblically solid responses to meaningful and relevant inquiries is essential. It should not be difficult for new believers or mature Christians to understand what it means to make a choice and declaration for Christ.

In the church, many people sit quietly with unanswered questions about what it means to be or become a Christian. When they receive responses, these answers are often unsatisfactory. This short book aims to provide clear and straightforward explanations of key aspects of being a Christian (believer) without excessive wording or complicated jargon.

This book came to fruition because of God's direction and guidance, fulfilling His determined purpose. As is common to His methodology, God motivated and inspired the writing and words in this book by His Spirit as time passed. Traditionally, when God has wanted to convey a message, edify, or bring clarification, He has moved by His spirit on the hearts and minds of faithful and available men to accomplish His purpose. The Bible is a clear and irrefutable example of this reality, written by 40 authors across several geographical locations, cultures, and periods over 1,600 years.

Undoubtedly, God is the same yesterday, today, and forever. He continues to inspire both men and women by His Spirit to build, edify, and perfect the body of Christ. This book is a testament to the truth that God can use anything we humbly place at His feet or in His hands. God has granted us various gifts and talents, and we are responsible for using those gifts to advance His Kingdom.

May we always remember that we have the choice to be vessels of honor for our God, suitable for the Master's use. Let us never forget that He is the potter, and we are the clay.

CHAPTER 1

WHAT DOES IT MEAN TO BE SAVED?

Romans 10:9-10, "If you openly declare that Jesus is Lord and believe in your heart that God raised him from the dead, you will be saved. For it is by believing in your heart that you are made right with God and by openly declaring your faith that you are saved."

What does it mean to be saved? This question has likely been posed by more Christians and non-Christians than any other inquiry related to the Christian faith. Responses to this question can vary across different denominations. However, the answer to this question, and all questions that arise in the hearts and minds of many, can be found in the pages of scripture. The Bible is the inerrant, infallible, and indisputable word of God. It speaks for itself, about itself, and needs nothing outside itself to explain itself. From beginning to end, the Word of God talks about him and what it means to follow Him.

The scriptures tell us in John 3:16-18, "For this is how God loved the world: He gave his one and only Son so that everyone who believes in him will not perish but have eternal life. God sent his Son into the world not to judge the world but to save the world through him. "There is no judgment against anyone who believes in him. But anyone who does not believe in him has already been judged for not believing in God's one and only Son."

The answer to the question posed is straightforward. To be saved means to believe in the Son, Jesus, whom God sent into the world. Anyone who believes in Him will receive eternal life. Being saved assures us that after our physical bodies pass away, we will live again upon Jesus's return. Additionally, we will not only live again, but we will also live forever with God and His Son, Jesus, in the eternal kingdom created by God, with foundations not made by human hands.

When we are saved, we experience a spiritual and positional transformation. God sees us as new creations once we receive the Lord's salvation. We become righteous in God's sight by receiving Christ as our Lord and Savior. We pass from darkness to light. More than that, we become adopted children of the living God.

Being Born Again

In the Synoptic Gospels, we encounter Nicodemus, a prominent member of the elite spiritual class and a respected religious leader and teacher. In John 3:3-7, Jesus addresses this Pharisee and ruler of the Jews, saying, "I tell you the truth, unless you are born again, you cannot see the Kingdom of God." Nicodemus responds with confusion, asking, "What do you mean? How can an old man go back into his mother's womb and be born again?" Jesus then replies, "I assure you; no one can enter the Kingdom of God without being born of water and the Spirit. Humans can reproduce only human life, but the Holy Spirit gives birth to spiritual life. So don't be surprised when I say, 'You must be born again.'"

Being born again refers to experiencing a spiritual rebirth. This rebirth is not physical; it is a transformation of the spirit. To be born again signifies a renewal that occurs within us, impacting our hearts, minds, and spirits. When we go through this process, our thoughts, motives, desires, and attitudes toward God and others are changed. Renewal is achieved through hope and faith in Christ Jesus alone. The change and renewal in our minds and hearts happen through hearing and reading the Word of God.

Through reading and studying God's word, we continue to grow in the knowledge of Christ and are regenerated daily. We have been born again—reborn of the Spirit—through the Holy Spirit. By the power of the Holy Spirit, we are renewed every day. We are justified in the eyes of God as soon as we accept Christ. However, sanctification is an ongoing process. As we walk with Christ Jesus and are led by the Holy Spirit, our old nature, character, and habits gradually fade, and we are made new. Since we have been born again, we have become more like Christ, who saved and redeemed, sanctifying us more and more with each passing day. Over time, our old selves diminish, and we are transformed into the new image of God. Jesus promised, "If you abide in me, I will abide in you."

CHAPTER 2

DO GOOD PEOPLE
GO TO HEAVEN?

Matthew 25:46, "Then they will go away to eternal punishment, but the righteous to eternal life."

The question of whether good people go to heaven is often raised by those who may not fully understand the teachings of the Bible. This inquiry can stem from a lack of in-depth study of the scriptures. However, it's natural to seek comfort in times of uncertainty, especially concerning deceased loved ones, family, and friends. The Bible answers this question clearly and explains who will enter heaven and the Kingdom of God.

The Bible clearly states that being considered "good" is not enough to enter heaven. Heaven is described as the Kingdom of God, a place for prepared people. Only those who have become children of God through Christ Jesus will enter the Kingdom. When Jesus was preparing to return to His Father in heaven, He reassured His disciples with these words recorded in John 14:1-3, "Don't let your hearts be troubled. Trust in God, and trust also in me. There is more than enough room in my father's home. If this were not so, would I have told you I would prepare a place for you? When everything is ready, I will come get you so you will always be with me where I am."

Unfortunately, only disciples and followers of the Lord Jesus Christ go to heaven. While morality, ethics, integrity, and outstanding character are undoubtedly desirable qualities, they are not enough to grant access to heaven. Only through Jesus Christ can we enter the Kingdom of God. There is no other way. No amount of work, good deeds, charity, or kind acts can earn us entry. Entrance to the Kingdom of God is only by accepting Jesus Christ and receiving Him as our Lord and personal Savior. Ephesians 2:8-9 reminds us, "God saved you by grace when you believed. And you can't take credit for this; it is a gift from God. Salvation is not a reward for our good deeds, so none of us can boast about it." Heaven cannot be earned. Even if we could live a perfect life but fail to put our trust, hope, and faith in Jesus, we would still face eternal separation from God, destined for a place initially prepared for the fallen angels: "Where their worm never dies, and the fire is not quenched" (Mark 9:48).

As believers and followers of Jesus, we are transformed by His Spirit. Through the power of the Holy Spirit, we become new creations and are guided to live better and more righteous lives than we did in the past. However, we understand that simply being "good" is not enough. God requires us to be perfect. Without Christ and the transforming power of the Holy Spirit, we cannot achieve righteousness in God's eyes. As stated in Romans 3:10-12, "No one is righteous—not even one. No one is wise; no one is seeking God. All have turned away; all have become useless. No one does good, not even one." Even when people referred to Him as "good," He replied in Mark 10:18, "Why do you call me good?" Jesus asked. "Only God is perfect."

Humanity, both men and women, is not inherently good. The only way to enter the Kingdom of God is through faith in Christ. Jesus clearly stated, "I am the way, the truth, and the life. No one comes to the Father except through me." He is the admission; He is the door. Without exception, we must all enter the Kingdom of God similarly. Heaven is reserved for the children of God—those who are sealed with His Spirit. Romans 2:11 reminds us, "There is no respect of persons with God." Only those who have been washed in the precious blood of the Lamb will one day joyfully see God face to face.

Good people do not go to heaven. We have no righteousness outside of Christ and cannot earn salvation. On the contrary, the scripture in Titus

3:5-7 tells us: "He saved us, not because of the righteous things we had done, but because of his mercy. He washed away our sins, giving us a new birth and life through the Holy Spirit. He generously poured the Spirit upon us through Jesus Christ, our Savior. Because of his grace, He made us right in his sight and gave us confidence that we would inherit eternal life."

CHAPTER 3

WHAT ARE WE SAVED FROM?

John 16:8, "When he comes, he will convict the world of
guilt concerning sin and righteousness and judgment."

According to biblical scripture, there is an explicit impending punishment and judgment awaiting a wicked, sinful, and unbelieving world. In 2 Peter 3:7-10, it is written: "The present heavens and earth have been reserved for fire, being kept for the day of judgment when ungodly people will be destroyed. But you must not forget this one thing, dear friends: a day is like a thousand years to the Lord, and a thousand years are like a day. The Lord isn't being slow in keeping His promise, as some people think. No, He is being patient for your sake. He does not want anyone to be destroyed but wants everyone to repent. However, the day of the Lord will come unexpectedly, like a thief. Then, the heavens will pass away with a loud noise, and the elements will disappear in fire. The earth and everything on it will be found deserving of judgment."

The Scriptures affirm that every person will stand before the holy and righteous God and ultimately face judgment after leaving this life. However, the Scriptures also teach that there is a clear distinction between the experiences and outcomes awaiting those who have placed their hope and faith in Christ and those who choose to reject Him through unbelief.

On that great day when all of humanity sees God, He will be a loving and compassionate Father or a holy and righteous Judge. How He receives us depends on our choice; God does not force anyone to accept Him. Instead, He allows us to either embrace or reject Him.

The Bible teaches that those saved and redeemed by Christ will stand before God's Bema (Mercy) seat on the final day. Their sins will have been wiped away and will never be remembered again. Every believer and follower of Christ has been justified and righteous in God's sight. The blood of the Lamb has cleansed them. Christ paid the penalty for their sins by shedding His precious and sacrificial blood on a lonely hill called Golgotha over 2,000 years ago. As they stand before the Bema seat of Christ, all believers will receive rewards for their faith in Him, their service to advance God's kingdom, and for living in a way that is pleasing and acceptable to Him.

In contrast, unbelievers will stand before the Great White Throne of Judgment in the presence of the all-powerful, all-knowing, and holy God. Those who have rejected Jesus, the LORD's Christ, will face God without an advocate. They will confront a perfect God who demands spiritual perfection and appear as defendants before a righteous, holy, and perfect Judge, held accountable for all their sins. They will be called to answer for their failure to achieve perfection and, more importantly, for their rejection of the only acceptable sacrifice for sin—the conscious and deliberate decision to turn away from the Savior of the world.

Undeniably, all men and women will one day leave this life and must account for their choices and decisions. Everyone will stand before the creator and unimaginable maker of the universe. Regarding that future day, the writer of Revelation 20:11-15 states: "And I saw a great white throne and the one sitting on it. The earth and sky fled from his presence, but they found no hiding place. I saw the great and small dead standing before God's throne. And the books were opened, including the Book of Life. The dead were judged according to their actions, as recorded in the books. The sea gave up its dead, and death and the grave gave up their dead. All were judged according to their deeds. Then, death and the grave were thrown into the lake of fire. This lake of fire is the second death. Anyone whose name was not found recorded in the Book of Life was thrown into the lake of fire."

CHAPTER 4

CAN ANYONE BE SAVED?

Romans 10:13: "Everyone who calls on the
name of the LORD will be saved."

Yes, potentially anyone can be saved. There is nothing God desires more than for all of humanity to be saved. The scriptures proclaim in 2 Peter 3:9, "The Lord isn't being slow about his promise to return, as some people think. No, he is being patient for your sake. He does not want anyone to perish, so he gives everyone more time to repent."

Anyone willing to confess their sins to God, acknowledge that Jesus Christ is Lord, and believe in their heart that God raised him from the dead can be saved. However, for many, this simple act can feel too difficult. They often believe they need to work or earn their way into heaven. Unfortunately for them, there is no way to earn the right or privilege to enter the Kingdom of God. Entrance is only through Jesus Christ, who offers this right as a free and priceless gift.

The scriptures indicate that God longs to rescue and save humanity. In John 3:16, we read, "For God so loved the world that he gave his only begotten Son, that whoever believes in Him shall not perish but have everlasting life." Additionally, Matthew 18:11-14 states: "For the Son of Man has come to save that which was lost. What do you think? If a man has a hundred sheep, and one of them goes astray, does he not leave the ninety-nine and go to the mountains to seek the lost one? And if he finds it, truly I say to you, he rejoices more over that sheep than the ninety-nine that did not go astray. Even so, it is not the will of your Father in heaven that one of these little ones should perish."

God does not want anyone to be lost. In Acts 4:11-12, we learn, "Jesus is the one referred to in the Scriptures, where it says, 'The stone that you builders rejected has now become the cornerstone.' There is salvation in no one else! God has given no other name under heaven by which we must be saved." This name given to all humanity for salvation is Jesus. The Apostle Paul writes in 1 Timothy 1:15, "This is a faithful saying and worthy of all acceptance: that Christ Jesus came into the world to save sinners, of whom I am chief." In 1 Timothy 2:4-6, it is stated, "For this is good and acceptable in the sight of God our Savior, who desires all people to be saved and to come to the knowledge of the truth. For there is one God and one mediator between God and men, Christ Jesus, who gave Himself a ransom for all."

God has provided an acceptable sacrifice for the atonement of sin in His graciousness: the man Christ Jesus, His only begotten Son. Anyone can be saved if they receive Jesus as their personal Savior. Romans 10:9 clearly outlines this: "For if you confess with your mouth that Jesus is Lord and believe in your heart that God raised Him from the dead, you will be saved, for it is by believing in your heart that you are made right with God and by confessing with your mouth that you are saved. As the Scriptures tell us, "Anyone who believes in Him will not be disappointed" (Romans 10:11).

CHAPTER 5

CAN WE EARN OR WORK FOR SALVATION?

Ephesians 2:8-9, "It is by grace you have been saved, through faith--and this not from yourselves, it is the gift of God, not by works, so that no one can boast."

Salvation cannot be earned. Many people believe that through their pious acts, rituals, self-denials, and religious routines, they can earn points with God, but they are seriously mistaken. Salvation cannot be earned because God will never share His praise with anyone. He had to make salvation a gift so that no person could boast about their accomplishments, rights, or personal merits. Humanity's ability to receive salvation had to be achieved through a means and standard that man cannot attain.

God recognized humanity's propensity for egotism, false piety, arrogance, competition, and elitism in His profound wisdom. As a result, He made reconciliation with Himself impossible through humanity's works, sacrifices, acts, and deeds of religious penance. Instead, He offered salvation as a gift to all who would accept and receive it through His son and Christ, Jesus.

Salvation cannot be attained through good deeds, charity, or random acts of extraordinary kindness. It cannot be achieved by hard work or busyness for good causes, even in the name of the Church, religious affiliations, or Christ. On the contrary, it can only be received through belief in the power of the redeeming work of Christ on the cross, as the Scriptures proclaim. The only way to obtain or receive salvation is through Christ. There is no other way!

If salvation could be earned through work, many would elevate themselves above others and see themselves as superior and deserving. Some might be denied salvation simply because they did not achieve the same significance level in their works as someone else. However, we are grateful for God's infinite wisdom and that this is not how He operates. Instead, He offers salvation as a gift, demonstrating His matchless and immeasurable love.

The writer states in Matthew 20:28, "The Son of Man did not come to be served but to serve and to give His life as a ransom for many." Additionally, John 3:15-18 explains, "Everyone who believes in Him will have eternal life. This is how God loved the world: He gave His only Son so that everyone who believes in Him will not perish but have eternal life. God sent His Son into the world not to judge the world but to save the world through Him. There is no judgment against anyone who believes in Him. However, anyone who does not believe in Him has already been judged for not believing in God's one and only Son."

God loves everyone, regardless of who they are; He shows no favoritism. All are welcome to come to Him. When asked about salvation, we find the following exchange recorded in Acts 16:30-31: "What must I do to be saved?" They replied, "Believe in the Lord Jesus Christ, and you will be saved, you and your household." Additionally, 1 John 2:2 states, "If you sin, there is someone to plead for you before the Father. He is Jesus Christ, the one who pleases God completely. He is the sacrifice for our sins, taking away not only our sins but the sins of the whole world." Furthermore, 1 John 4:14 and 5:12 declare, "We have seen with our own eyes and now testify that the Father sent His Son to be the Savior of the world... So, whoever has God's Son has life; whoever does not have His Son does not have eternal life."

CHAPTER 6

HOW ARE WE SAVED?

Hebrews 10:39 says, "We are not of those who shrink back (in unbelief) and are destroyed, but of those who believe (in Christ) and are saved."

Many people have asked the question, "How are we saved?" The Bible provides a clear answer: all humanity can be saved through Jesus Christ. He states, "I am the way, the truth, and the life. No one comes to the Father except through me." With these words, Jesus, the Son of God and the second person of the Trinity proclaims that He is the way to salvation. The power of God saves us through Jesus, who rescues us from the destruction that awaits those who reject and refuse to believe in Him, the one faithful Savior of the world. We must place our faith in Christ Jesus alone to enter the Kingdom of God.

Salvation is available to all men and women solely through Christ Jesus. There is no other source of salvation. Only Christ can save us. Without accepting Him, individuals remain lost and desperate in their sins. The scriptures state in Mark 16:15-16: "He said to them, 'Go into all the world and preach the gospel (good news) to every creature. He who believes that I, Jesus, died to pay the price for their sins and rose again—who understands that I am the only acceptable sacrifice for the sins of all humanity—will be saved, but he who does not believe will be condemned." Without Christ, all humanity faces condemnation. Only the blood of Christ can redeem us, cleanse us, and satisfy the penalty for sin. As the hymn asks, "What can wash away my sins?" The answer remains unchanged: nothing but the blood of Jesus!

God is gracious, loving, and eternally kind. Since no human can be perfect and wholly righteous, the Eternal One provided a way for complete redemption through His Son. The writer tells us in John 3:17, "God did not send His Son into the world to condemn the world, but that the world through Him might be saved." In John 10:9, Jesus declared, "I am the door. If anyone enters by Me, he will be saved and will go in and out and find pasture."

Christ is the only acceptable advocate for those who are depraved, sin-stained, and lost. The author of Acts 4:12 clearly states, "There is salvation (deliverance and forgiveness from the penalty of sin) in no one else, for there is no other name under heaven given among men by which we must be saved." When asked by his disciples, "Sirs, what must I do to be saved?" they responded, "Believe in the Lord Jesus Christ, and you will be saved, you and your household" (Acts 16:30-31).

We are saved by believing in Jesus and what the Scriptures say about Him. To attain salvation, we must firmly believe that Jesus is the only faithful Savior of the world. We must believe He died on the cross, was buried in a borrowed tomb, and rose from the dead three days later. Romans 10:9 tells us, "If you confess with your mouth that Jesus is Lord and believe in your heart that God raised Him from the dead, you will be saved."

God does not have favorites and shows no favoritism. He is loving and kind to everyone. Anyone who comes to Him will be accepted and never be turned away. The scriptures state in 1 Corinthians, "The message of the cross is foolishness to those who are perishing, but to us who are being saved, it is the power of God." Regardless of how foolish it may seem, all men and women must come to Christ for salvation. There are no substitutes or alternatives. The scriptures are clear: there is no other way to be saved from the punishment and penalty of sin except through the gift of eternal life, which is available only through Christ Jesus. The writer declares in 1 Timothy 2:5, "There is one God and one Mediator who can reconcile God and humanity—the man Christ Jesus."

CHAPTER 7

WHO SAVED US AND WHY?

Philippians 3:20-21, "We are citizens of heaven, where
the Lord Jesus Christ lives. And we are eagerly waiting for
him to return as our Savior. He will change our weak mortal
bodies into glorious bodies like his own, using the same power
with which he will bring everything under his control."

Who saved us and why? Jesus Christ and no one else save us. He has
saved us out of His incredible love for us. The work of our salvation
is solely His. We cannot save ourselves or perform any actions or duties to
earn salvation. It cannot be achieved through our efforts. Our salvation
results from Christ's selfless act of dying on the cross.

Before the world began, Christ Jesus decided to come into the world,
die, and pay the price for our ransom to set us free, purely because He
loved us. He saved us because only He could. As stated in Titus 3:5, "Not
by works of righteousness which we have done, but according to His
mercy, He (Jesus) saved us, by the washing of regeneration and renewing
of the Holy Spirit." Similarly, 1 Timothy 2:5-6 tells us, "For there is one
God, and one mediator between God and men, the man Christ Jesus, who
gave Himself a ransom for all, to be testified in due time."

The author of Ephesians 2:8-9 highlights that "God saved you by His
grace when you believed in Christ Jesus. You can't take credit for this; it

is a gift from God. Salvation is not a reward for our good deeds, so none of us can boast about it." This means we have not done anything to gain, earn, or contribute to our salvation. It is solely and entirely the work of a loving and gracious God.

Ephesians 2:13-14 18 states, "Now you have been united with Christ Jesus. Once, you were far away from God, but now you have been brought near to Him through the blood of Christ, for Christ Himself has brought peace to us. He united Jews and Gentiles into one people when, in His own body on the cross, He broke down the wall of hostility that separated us. Now all of us can come to the Father through the same Holy Spirit because of what Christ has done for us."

Jesus's atoning blood saves us. Because He died on the cross at Calvary over two thousand years ago, we can choose to receive Him as both Lord and Savior, along with His gift of eternal life. The Scriptures clearly state that salvation can be found in no one else but Jesus alone. Philippians 2:6-11 says concerning Jesus: "Though he was God, he did not think of equality with God as something to cling to. Instead, he gave up his divine privileges; he took the humble position of a slave and was born as a human being. When he appeared in human form, he humbled himself in obedience to God and died a criminal's death on the cross. Therefore, God elevated him to the place of highest honor and gave him the name above all other names, that in the name of Jesus, every knee should bow, in heaven and on earth and under the earth, and every tongue declare that Jesus Christ is Lord, to the glory of God the Father." Furthermore, the Scripture highlights the words of Jesus in John 6:47-48: "I tell you the truth, anyone who believes (in Me) has eternal life. Yes, I am the bread of life!"

CHAPTER 8

IS EVERYONE SAVED OR GOING TO BE SAVED?

1 Corinthians 1:18, "The message of the cross is foolishness to those who are perishing, but to us who are being saved, it is the power of God."

It is good and reasonable to ask as many questions as possible, especially regarding where we, our friends, acquaintances, and loved ones might spend eternity. When we consider that we all exit this present reality and must eventually return to our Creator, it is only natural to inquire about our salvation and that of others. Whether everyone will be saved or ultimately attain salvation is profound. The answer to this question and all others like it can be found in the scriptures.

The scriptures answer whether everyone is saved or will be saved. From scripture, we can see that although God is full of love, tenderness, kindness, and boundless mercy, not everyone is or will be saved. While every person has the potential for salvation, many do not choose it. All have access and the opportunity to come to Christ, the source of salvation. However, many reject Him. Whether one is saved or not ultimately comes down to personal choice. Every man and woman can come to Christ and receive the gift offered through Him.

The writer emphasizes this in John 6:35-40: "Jesus replied, 'I am the bread of life. Whoever comes to me will never be hungry again. Whoever believes in me will never be thirsty. But you haven't believed in me even though you have seen me. However, those the Father has given me will come to me, and I will never reject them. I have come down from heaven to do the will of God who sent me, not to do my own will. And this is the will of God, that I should not lose even one of all those He has given me, but that I should raise them at the last day, for it is my Father's will that all who see His Son and believe in Him should have eternal life. I will raise them on the last day."

God has made a way for humanity—not just a select few—to be saved and reconciled with the perfect, righteous, and holy God. He sacrificed His only Son, Jesus, the second person of the Trinity, to atone for the sins of all people. John 3:16-21 highlights God's selfless demonstration of love toward humanity, stating, "For God loved the world so much that he gave his one and only Son so that everyone who believes in him will not perish but have eternal life. God sent his Son into the world not to judge the world but to save the world through him. There is no judgment against anyone who believes in him, but anyone who does not believe in him has already been judged for not believing in God's one and only Son. This judgment is based on this fact: God's light came into the world, but people loved the darkness more than the light because their actions were evil. All who do evil hate the light and refuse to go near it, fearing their sins will be exposed. But those who do what is right come to the light so that others can see what they are doing is what God wants."

Due to His unmatched and unearned love, tenderness, and kindness, God extended incredible grace toward humanity, even when people were unaware of their need for a Savior. Romans 5:8 states, "God demonstrates His love toward us, in that while we were still sinners, Christ died for us." Many individuals see themselves as generally good, leading them to believe they do not need a Savior. They fail to recognize that they possess no righteousness apart from God, who demands perfection. As a result, they can be deceived, resistant, and tend to dispute God's infallible word. Most people do not see themselves as sinners and do not understand that anything short of perfection is unacceptable to God. Humanity lacks the righteousness that meets God's standards. Romans 3:23 reminds us, "All have sinned and fall short of God's glory (the standard of perfection)."

God is perfect and calls us to strive for perfection. In Matthew 5:48, we are instructed, "You are to be perfect, even as your Father in heaven is perfect." This call to perfection refers not to human perfection but to spiritual perfection, which can only be achieved through a relationship with God through Christ Jesus.

No one can be saved unless they first recognize and confess their need for a Savior. It is essential to understand that without Christ, our Savior, we remain in our sins and are eternally separated from God. Only those willing to acknowledge the truth about their depravity and invite Jesus into their hearts as both Lord and Savior can and will be saved.

Sadly, many people reject and deny their need for a Savior, as well as freedom and deliverance from sin. They do not see themselves as bad people or sinners. Consequently, they refuse to acknowledge Jesus as the only Savior and deny their need for His saving grace, mercy, and power in their lives. Concerning those who reject Him and their need for Him, Jesus states in Mark 2:17, "Those who are well (or believe they are) do not need a physician, but those who are sick (acknowledging their illness as a result of sin): I did not come to call the righteous (those who consider themselves so), but sinners to turn away from sin and choose eternal life through repentance in Me." The belief that we possess goodness or righteousness apart from God contradicts the message of 1 Timothy 4:10, which explains that we are saved "because we trust in the living God, who is the Savior of all men, especially of those who believe."

According to the scriptures, Jesus physically represents the invisible God. He is God the Son, who entered the world in human form through a virgin birth. The writer of 1 Timothy 3:16 states, "God was manifested (revealed) in the flesh (Jesus), justified in the Spirit, seen by angels, preached to the Gentiles, believed on in the world, and taken up into glory (heaven)."

Furthermore, John 1:1-2 states, "In the beginning (before the world was formed) was the Word, and the Word was with God, and the Word was God (not a god). The Word (Christ) became flesh and dwelled among us, and we (humanity) beheld His glory, the glory of the only begotten of the Father, full of grace and truth."

In Romans 10: 9-13, the scriptures declare inarguably, "If you openly declare that Jesus is Lord and believe in your heart that God raised him from the dead, you will be saved, for it is by believing in your heart that you are made right with God and by openly declaring your faith that you are saved. As the Scriptures tell us, "Anyone who trusts in him will never be disgraced." Jews and Gentiles are the same in this respect. They have the same Lord, who gives generously to all who call on him. "Everyone who calls on the name of the Lord will be saved." Only those who believe in Him will be saved.

CHAPTER 9

CAN WE LOSE OUR SALVATION?

John 10:27-30, "My sheep hear my voice, and I know them, and they follow me: And I give unto them eternal life, and they shall never perish, neither shall any man pluck them out of my hand. My Father, which gave them me, is greater than all, and no man can pluck them out of my Father's hand. My Father and I are one."

I s it possible to lose our salvation? This question can be addressed directly through biblical scriptures. The scriptures indicate that a believer—a spirit-filled follower of the Lord Jesus—is entirely justified, regenerated, and eternally secure in their salvation. Their security comes from faith in Christ's atoning work on the cross, meaning they cannot lose their salvation. While some disagree, the Bible does not support the idea that salvation can be lost. Rather than focusing solely on whether salvation can be lost, it is more important to consider whether a person was genuinely saved in the first place.

The Bible contains several scriptures that reinforce the belief that we are eternally secure in Christ once we are born again. The writer in Isaiah 43:25 states, "I, even I, am he who blots out your transgressions for my own sake, and I will not remember your sins." Similarly, Jeremiah 31:34 declares, "They will no longer teach their neighbor or say to one another, 'Know the LORD,' because they will all know me, from the least of them to the greatest," declares the LORD. "For I will forgive their wickedness and remember their sins no more."

Other scriptures support this idea. We read in Hebrews 8:12, "For I will be merciful to their unrighteousness, and their sins and their iniquities I will remember no more." Additionally, Hebrews 10:17 echoes this sentiment, stating, "And their sins and iniquities I will remember no more."

If salvation is a gift, God wishes to save us more than punish us. The scriptures consistently communicate this message: God's forgiveness is absolute. When God forgives, our sins are eternally forgiven and forgotten. Once forgiven, our sins are cast into the sea of forgetfulness, never to be remembered or held against us again.

To save humanity, God provided a ransom to pay the price and penalty for sin: Jesus Christ, the Son of God. By taking on the penalty for all sin, He offers freedom to humanity, but it requires that individuals receive Him as their Savior. As the acceptable sacrifice, God asks that Christ be acknowledged as the only Lord and Savior. In doing so, the penalty for all sins—past, present, and future—is satisfied.

In John 3:16, the writer states, "For God so loved the world that he gave his one and only Son, that whoever believes in him shall not perish but have eternal life." This scripture emphasizes that anyone who accepts and believes in Christ as the Messiah will be saved. The death of Jesus on the cross fulfilled the requirement for all sins once and for all. Nothing can be added to this unparalleled work; it is sufficient and complete.

Supporting this idea, the writer in Colossians 2:13-14 says, "You were dead in your sins and the uncircumcision of your sinful nature; God made you alive with Christ. He forgave us all our sins, having canceled the charge of our legal indebtedness, which stood against us and condemned us; he has taken it away, nailing it to the cross."

Salvation is an act of grace; it is a gift from God that we do not deserve. Because of His love, God offers salvation to all through Christ Jesus alone, and no salvation is found in anyone else. Jesus is the Way, the Truth, and the Life. He came into the world to redeem all of humanity. Once we are in Christ, we belong to Him for eternity. In John 6:37-39, Jesus states: "All that the Father gives Me will come to Me, and whoever comes to Me I will never cast out. I did not come down from heaven to do My own will but to fulfill the will of Him who sent Me. This is the will of the Father who sent Me: I should lose nothing of all He has given Me, but I should raise it again on the last day." Additionally, John 10:28 states, "I give them eternal life, and they shall never perish; no one will snatch them out of My hand."

In Romans 8:38-39, the Apostle Paul emphasizes our eternal security in Christ. He states, "I am convinced that neither death nor life, nor angels, nor principalities, nor powers, nor present things, nor things to come, nor height, nor depth, nor any other created thing will be able to separate us from the love of God, which is in Christ Jesus our Lord."

In Ephesians 2:8-9 and 4:30, the writer also reminds us, "For by grace you have been saved through faith, and that not of yourselves; it is the gift of God, not of works, lest anyone should boast... And do not grieve the Holy Spirit of God, by whom you were sealed for the day of redemption."

Finally, Hebrews 10:12-14 declares, "But this Man, after He had offered one sacrifice for sins forever, sat down at the right hand of God; from that time waiting till His enemies are made His footstool. For by one offering, He has perfected those being sanctified forever."

CHAPTER 10

CAN WE BE CERTAIN THAT WE ARE SAVED?

John 5:24, "I tell you the truth, those who listen to my message and believe in God who sent me have eternal life. They will never be condemned for their sins, but they have already passed from death into life.

M any people have raised concerns about their salvation. It is common to ask, "Can we be certain that we are saved?" This question is not only valid but also very important. Our spiritual condition should be a priority and of significant interest, as it will undeniably have eternal consequences.

The scriptures provide the best source for finding answers to all spiritual questions. As children of God, we are people of the Book. We are guided, directed, and instructed by God's word, especially regarding spiritual matters. As stated in 2 Timothy 3:16-17, "All Scripture is inspired by God and is useful to teach us what is true and to make us aware of what is wrong in our lives. It corrects us when we are wrong and teaches us to do what is right. God uses it to prepare and equip His people to do every good work."

We can have assurance of our salvation based on what God has declared and promised in His Word. The scriptures tell us that salvation is not merely a feeling but a deep, abiding sense of knowing. We are assured because we have placed our trust, hope, and faith in Christ Jesus, our only hope for salvation. The scriptures instruct those justified to live by faith, for we cannot please our great God without faith.

In John 10:28-29, our Savior assures us of our salvation, stating, "I give them eternal life, and they will never perish. No one can snatch them away from me, for my Father has given them to me, and he is more powerful than anyone else. No one can snatch them from the Father's hand."

If we lack the faith to believe and trust in God, we essentially call Him a liar, suggesting that He is unfaithful and unable to uphold His Word and fulfill His promises. However, God cannot lie. Because of His righteous nature and unchanging character, we can trust Him and the assurance of His Word without exception.

The Scriptures indicate no prerequisites or strict requirements for receiving the gift of salvation. The only requirement is faith in Jesus, the LORD's Christ. Since we cannot earn salvation, we must accept it as a gift. Our assurance of salvation is based on our willingness to believe what the Scriptures declare about Jesus and the power of His precious shed blood.

The scriptures convey a powerful message in John 1:10-12: "He (Christ Jesus) came into the very world He created, but the world didn't recognize Him. He came to His own people, and even they rejected Him. However, to all who believed in Him and accepted Him, He gave the right to become children of God."

Furthermore, in John 10:9-11 it is written about Jesus, "He explained it to them: "Yes, I am the gate. Those who come in through Me will be saved. They will come and go freely and will find good pastures. The thief's purpose is to steal, kill, and destroy. My purpose is to give them a rich and satisfying life. I am the good shepherd. The good shepherd sacrifices His life for the sheep."

If we believe in Christ and find comfort in the truth of the Scriptures, we can be confident that we are saved and continually being saved. Because our hope is in Christ, nothing can separate us from God's love, hand, and security. As stated in John 5:24, "I tell you the truth, whoever hears my message and believes in God who sent me has eternal life. They will never be condemned for their sins; they have crossed from death to life."

CHAPTER 11

CAN WE HAVE CONFIDENCE OF OUR SALVATION?

Mark 16:17-18, "These signs will accompany those who believe: In my name, they will drive out demons; they will speak in new tongues; they will pick up snakes with their hands; and when they drink deadly poison, it will not hurt them at all; they will place their hands on sick people, and they will get well."

Can we be confident that we are saved? This is an essential and reasonable question to consider. According to the Scriptures, clear signs and evidence in a believer's life assure salvation. One significant indication of our conversion is our desire to fellowship with the Savior whenever possible. This includes praying, studying His Word, engaging in quiet meditation and reflection, and spending time with other redeemed believers.

Before the Spirit of Christ entered our lives, our priorities were different. As stated in Ephesians 5:8, "Once you were full of darkness, but now you have light from the Lord. So, live as people of light! This light within you produces only what is good and right and true."

Another proof that we have been saved and redeemed by the Savior is that those around us can see and testify to the marked and apparent change in us and how we conduct ourselves compared to the past. Now that Christ has come into our hearts, we more than talk the talk; we walk the walk. How we live our lives makes us worthy of the moniker "Christian" because we look like Christ through the spirit of God.

We are assured of our salvation because, unlike in the past, we strive to correct our wrongs, confess our faults, accept insults rather than dish them out, and work diligently to be gentle and kind while seeking peace with everyone. This transformation is made possible only through the power of the Holy Spirit, who now resides within us.

We know we are saved when we surrender, yield, and obey God's voice and word. By listening to God's voice and following the guidance of His Spirit—obeying the instructions, corrections, and teachings given to us as His children—we demonstrate that we are legitimate sons and daughters of God. One of the most profound proofs of our regeneration is our obedience. Obeying God reflects our fellowship with Him and our love for Him.

We know that we have been changed and renewed by the spirit of God because now, we walk in the newness of life. We have abandoned old habits, patterns, and behaviors. With intentionality, purpose, and commitment, we strive to live and conduct our lives in a manner that demonstrates our worthiness to be called followers of Christ and brings honor to God. The writer says in Ephesians 2:13, "You have been united with Christ Jesus. Once you were far away from God, but now you have been brought near to him through the blood of Christ."

We know we belong to Him because we follow His ways and love Him and His people. We have passed from death to life, willingly sharing everything with other believers and embodying Jesus' teachings on selflessness and humility. In John 13:12-17 and 34-35, Jesus teaches us: "You call Me 'Teacher' and 'Lord,' and you are right. Since I have washed your feet, you should wash each other's feet. I give you a new commandment: Love each other as I have loved you. Your love for one another will prove to the world that you are My disciples."

The apostle Paul provides one of the most evident indications of our conversion. He teaches that we know we have been changed when love is apparent. Where God resides, there is Agape—unconditional love.

The Bible instructs us to "love our neighbors as we love ourselves." Only through the Spirit of the living God can we genuinely love those who are sometimes difficult to love. When we feel a sincere desire and willingness to follow the command to "love," we can be confident that we have been born again.

The scripture outlines several ways to affirm our conversion, as highlighted in Galatians 5:22. As individuals filled with the Spirit of God, we will begin to display righteous characteristics due to the transformative work of the Holy Spirit within us. We have become new creations, and our old habits and practices are fading, making room for a new life.

As new beings, we now produce different fruits. Galatians says, "The fruit of the Spirit is love, joy, peace, longsuffering, gentleness, goodness, faith, meekness, temperance: against such there is no law. Those who belong to Christ have crucified the flesh with its passions and desires. If we live in the Spirit, let us also walk in the Spirit." Our love for one another and the fruit we bear prove that we are Christians and are saved.

CHAPTER 12

WHAT HAPPENS TO THE UNSAVED?

2 Peter 2:4, 6, "If God did not spare angels when they sinned, but sent them to hell, putting them into gloomy dungeons to be held for judgment; if he condemned the cities of Sodom and Gomorrah by burning them to ashes, and made them an example of what is going to happen to the ungodly."

What happens to those who are unsaved, meaning those who reject and deny the saving power of Christ Jesus? Although difficult for many to accept, the answer is clear and undeniable. The unsaved will live in eternity, separated from God. They will spend eternity in a place that was initially prepared for the disobedient and fallen angels who participated in the Luciferian Rebellion against God. However, because humanity has intentionally chosen to reject God's offer of reconciliation, Hell has expanded to accommodate the souls of those who turn away from Him. The scriptures confirm this in Matthew 25:41: "Then the King will turn to those on His left and say, 'Away with you, you cursed ones, into the eternal fire prepared for the devil and his demons.'"

Many people prefer to reject or deny the existence of a place of torment, punishment, or retribution meant for those who deny and reject Christ. However, the reality of such a place is explicitly and undeniably described in scripture and is not a mere imagination. Although many are reluctant to acknowledge the existence of this place of punishment, that unwillingness does not diminish its reality. Individuals—both men and women—will be separated from God because they reject Christ. Many find it difficult to see God as someone who would inflict such punishment. Most people prefer to view God as all-loving, gentle, and kind, emphasizing His forgiving nature rather than recognizing Him as a holy and sovereign king who demands a standard of holiness and righteousness.

God does not send anyone to hell; humanity chooses separation through continuous acts of defiance and disobedience. Hell is a real place, despite the denial of those who deceive themselves. Scripture tells us that hell is real. Luke 16:19-28 states: "There was a rich man dressed in purple and fine linen and enjoyed a lavish lifestyle daily. At his gate, there was a beggar named Lazarus, who was covered in sores. Eventually, the beggar died and was carried by angels to Abraham's side. The rich man also died and was buried. In hell, the rich man raised his eyes and, in torment, saw Abraham far away with Lazarus at his side. He cried out, "Father Abraham, have mercy on me. Send Lazarus to dip the tip of his finger in water and cool my tongue, for I am in agony in this flame." He continued, "I ask you, father, to send him to my father's house, for I have five brothers. Let him warn them so they don't end up in this place of torment."

Hell is real, but no one is meant to go there. God desires that no one perishes. However, scripture is clear: unless we are born again and the Spirit of Christ lives in us, we do not belong to Him and cannot see God. Without Christ, no one can be born again or receive salvation. Jesus emphasized, "I am the Way, the Truth, and the Life." He paid the price and penalty for sin. Through Christ Jesus, everyone can be born again. The scriptures affirm in John 3:16: "God so loved the world that He gave His only begotten Son, that whosoever believes in Him should not perish, but have everlasting life." Anyone who goes to hell does so by their own choice. He or she rejects Christ, the only hope and way of salvation.

God desires that all be saved, and He has made every effort to ensure this possibility. Loving humanity with such overwhelming love, He took on humanity, wrapped himself in the flesh, came into the world, and paid the penalty for sin, freeing humankind from the debt they could not pay. The scriptures state in John 1:10-14: "He came into the very world He created, but the world did not recognize Him. He came to His own people, and even they rejected Him. However, to all who believed in Him and accepted Him, He gave them the right to become children of God. These individuals are reborn—not through a physical birth resulting from human passion or planning, but through a birth that comes from God. Therefore, the Word became human and made His home among us. He was full of unfailing love and faithfulness, and we have seen His glory, the glory of the Father's one and only Son."

The unsaved are lost and separated from God, not because salvation is unavailable, but because they deliberately, intentionally, and willfully reject Christ. They reject the source of life, the only hope they have for redemption and reconciliation with God. Although Christ makes the invitation open to all, many refuse to accept and embrace it. The scriptures tell us in Luke 15:7, "There is more joy in heaven over one lost sinner who repents and returns to God than over ninety-nine others who are righteous and haven't strayed away!"

The unsaved receive punishment, not because God desires to punish. On the contrary, they are rewarded for their evil deeds, desires, actions, and rebellion. Through Christ Jesus, the saved choose to obey God, receiving His Spirit and walking in it. Speaking of this, the writer says in Romans 6:22-23, "Now you are free from the power of sin and have become slaves of God. Now, you do those things that lead to holiness and eternal life. For the wages of sin is death, but the gift of God is eternal life through Christ Jesus our Lord."

Following the Lord in obedience, the saved manifest the fruit of regeneration through Christ. Affirming the fruit of the Spirit, the writer in Galatians 5 says, "The Holy Spirit produces this kind of fruit in our lives: love, joy, peace, patience, kindness, goodness, faithfulness, gentleness, and self-control. There is no law against these things! Those who belong to Christ Jesus have nailed the passions and desires of their sinful nature to his cross and crucified them there. Since we live by the Spirit, let us follow the Spirit's leadership in every part of our lives. Let us not become conceited, or provoke one another, or be jealous of one another."

In contrast, Galatians 5 describes the continuous and habitual behaviors of the unsaved. The saved strive to walk in the Spirit of Christ and adhere to His will and standards, while the unsaved reject Christ, and their actions are evident. Galatians 5:17-21 states about the unsaved, "The sinful nature wants to do evil, which is just the opposite of what the Spirit wants. And the Spirit gives us desires contrary to what the sinful nature desires. These two forces are constantly in conflict, making carrying out your good intentions difficult. However, when the Spirit leads you, you are not subject to the law of Moses. The consequences of following the desires of your sinful nature are apparent: sexual immorality, impurity, lustful pleasures, idolatry, sorcery, hostility, quarreling, jealousy, outbursts of anger, selfish ambition, dissension, division, envy, drunkenness, wild parties, and other sins like these. I warn you again, as I have before that anyone living this kind of life will not inherit the Kingdom of God."

In 2 Corinthians 5:21, it is stated, "God made Christ, who never sinned, to be the offering for our sin so that we could be made right with God through Christ." Christ took on the penalty for all so that none would have to face eternal punishment. However, many choose to reject His gift of salvation. Because of this reality, the writer warns in Galatians 6:7-8, "Don't be misled—you cannot mock the justice of God. You will always harvest what you plant. Those who live only to satisfy their sinful nature will harvest decay and death from that nature. But those who live to please the Spirit will harvest everlasting life from the Spirit."

CHAPTER 13

WHAT DOES IT MEAN TO BE A CHRISTIAN?

1 Peter 4:16, "However, if you suffer as a Christian, do not be ashamed, but praise God that you bear that name."

The term "Christian" was first used to describe the believers and followers of Christ in Antioch, as noted in Acts 11:26: "The disciples were called Christians first in Antioch." Initially, "Christian" did not carry a sense of pride; instead, it was associated with dishonor, mockery, and negative connotations. Before being called Christians, followers of the Lord Jesus were referred to as those or people of "The Way," reflecting Jesus' statement: "I AM the way, the truth, and the life." Therefore, Christians are followers of "The Way."

Being a Christian means following Jesus Christ and accepting Him as Lord and Savior. It involves having faith, hope, and trust in Christ alone as our redeemer, advocate, and reconciler to God. To be a Christian implies a surrender to Him and an unwavering conviction that Jesus is the source of life, the Son of God, and the only acceptable sacrifice for saving humanity from the penalty of sin, as He died on the cross at Calvary.

As Christians, we have consciously chosen to embrace the teachings of the Lord Jesus. We affirm that Christ Jesus is the only Savior for a dying and unbelieving world, and we commit to being His ambassadors and representatives on Earth. We willingly accept the possibility of suffering for the sake of the Gospel message, just as our predecessors have done—even to the point of death. Being a Christian means being prepared to pay the ultimate price, if necessary, to proclaim the truth of the Gospel.

As Christians, we believe and embrace the Bible as the Word of God. We affirm that the messages about Christ found in the Old and New Testaments are valid and that every promise regarding the future is guaranteed. As followers of Christ, we recognize the Scriptures' call for us to be both hearers and doers of God's Word. Because of this, we are compelled to share the truth of God's Word and address humanity's need for a Savior, Jesus, in their lives. Jesus said in John 3:36, "Anyone who believes in God's Son has eternal life. Anyone who doesn't obey the Son will never experience eternal life but remains under God's angry judgment." Therefore, we must boldly proclaim the truth of Christ.

Being a Christian means that our old nature has passed away, and we have embraced the nature and spirit of Christ. As followers of Christ, we strive daily to be transformed more and more into the image of God, becoming increasingly like Him. As His disciples, God's Spirit operates in our lives, guiding us to serve Him and accomplish His chosen work. As people of "The Way," we recognize that He alone is God. We are His creation, and He has the right to use us as He sees fit. He is our Father; we are His children. He is our Redeemer, reconciler, and the Lord and Master of our lives.

As Christians, we no longer live or think as we once did. Our minds, ideas, attitudes, and perspectives have changed. The Spirit of God now guides us and has given us the mind of Christ. Our thoughts and viewpoints are closely intertwined with God and His Word. We identify as people of the Book and are reminded in 2 Corinthians 5:17: "If anyone is in Christ, he is a new creation; old things have passed away; behold, all things have become new." God's Word governs our lives; we are all called to be God's disciples and ministers (servants).

CHAPTER 14

I AM A CHRISTIAN. NOW WHAT?

John 8:12, "When Jesus spoke again to the people, he
said, I am the light of the world. Whoever follows me will
never walk in darkness but will have the light of life".

Once we become Christians, we acknowledge that we have accepted Jesus as our Lord and Savior, recognizing His sovereignty and supremacy in every aspect of our lives. Having welcomed Christ and invited Him into our hearts, we no longer have the right or privilege to live as we choose; we now belong to Him. He is our Master, and we are His servants. As followers of the Lord Christ, we are commanded to obey Him and do His will. Specifically, we are instructed to "go" into the world and preach the gospel—the good news about Christ—to people everywhere, regardless of their nation, tribe, ethnicity, or cultural background.

Because we have accepted Christ into our hearts, He has given us His Spirit, who now lives within us. Without the Holy Spirit working within us, we cannot fulfill the tasks He has called us to do. However, since He resides in us, we can achieve anything. Nothing is impossible for those who believe. Now that we belong to Him, He will consistently help, care, and provide for us. Without a petition, He will protect, guide, and shield us during times of hardship and desperation. Because He has adopted us, we have assurance that He will never leave us alone, abandoned, or orphaned. We are His children, and He is a loving and compassionate Father.

As Christians, we are part of the body of Christ, belonging to a global family of believers dedicated to pleasing God and fulfilling His will. Collectively, we are an imperfect family. However, the same Spirit is at work, transforming us not the image of God moment by moment and day by day.

As believers and followers of Christ, we are part of a unique and special group—we belong to the family of the living God. While he creates all of humanity, not everyone is considered His child. Unlike many others, we have been adopted into God's family, the universe's sovereign. The writer of Ephesians 1:4-7 tells us, "Even before he made the world, God loved us and chose us in Christ to be holy and without fault in his eyes. God adopted us into his family by bringing us to Himself through Jesus Christ. He wanted to do this, and it gave him great pleasure. So, we praise God for the glorious grace he has poured out on us who belong to his dear Son. He is so rich in kindness and grace that he purchased our freedom with the blood of his Son and forgave our sins." We are the children of God, seeds of righteousness, temporary citizens of earth, eagerly awaiting the promised eternal Kingdom of God. We have been redeemed at an immeasurable price—the shed blood of Jesus Christ, the Lamb of God.

We have been called by God and chosen to represent our Lord and Savior. As His emissaries and ambassadors, we are expected to teach, preach, and reach the lost with the redeeming message of Christ. Our mission is twofold: to bring Christ to men and women and to bring men and women to Christ. To fulfill this purpose, God has given every believer the Holy Spirit, who empowers us and is always available to help. The Holy Spirit leads, guides, and directs us in our efforts. The scriptures outline the Holy Spirit's role, function, and operation. In 1 Corinthians 12:4-11, we are told there are various spiritual gifts from the same Spirit. While we serve different roles, we all serve the same Lord. God works in many ways, but God accomplishes His work in each of us similarly. Every person receives a spiritual gift to help others. Some are given wise counsel, others special knowledge, great faith, healing, and the ability to perform miracles or to prophesy. Some can discern messages from God, speak in unknown languages, or interpret them. The Spirit distributes these gifts as He sees fit, deciding which gifts each person should have. Through the Holy Spirit, we are equipped and strengthened to carry out our mission in the world.

As Christians, we are called to be a shining light in an increasingly dark world. We are encouraged to allow the Spirit of God to shape us into the likeness of our Savior, Christ Jesus. Jesus went about doing good by feeding the hungry, healing the sick, raising the dead, casting out demons, teaching the Scriptures, encouraging others, instructing, fasting, praying, and demonstrating God's power in all that He did. Consistently, the Savior brought honor and glory to God, and we are expected to do the same.

As children of the Savior, we are seeds of righteousness and citizens of both the temporal earth and the anticipated eternal Kingdom of God. We are no longer our own to do as we please; we have been purchased at an immeasurable price—the shed blood of Jesus Christ, the Lamb of God. As followers and disciples of Jesus, we are responsible for fulfilling His mandate: "Go and make disciples of all nations."

As ambassadors of Christ, we are called to preach and teach the truth of God's Word, sharing the hope and life that can only be found in Christ Jesus. There is no greater goal or objective than this. Christ not only expects but demands that we share our faith, hope, and trust in Him with others. Each of us is tasked with the work of an evangelist, sharing our testimonies with those who have never heard the Gospel—the good news of Jesus Christ. Without exception, we must represent our Savior and Lord, honoring our Father by proclaiming to every creature the undeniable truth of Christ's death, burial, and resurrection, along with His precious blood's redeeming and transformative power.

CHAPTER 15

WHAT TO EXPECT AS A CHRISTIAN!

1 Peter 2:16, "However, if you suffer as a Christian, do not be ashamed, but praise God that you bear that name."

What should Christians expect when choosing to follow Christ? This question is intriguing and complex, but the scriptures provide valuable insights. Undoubtedly, we can anticipate experiences unique to those who call on the name of Christ. As followers of Christ, we can expect far more spectacular, adventurous, and vibrant lives than we may have imagined. Being granted the right, privilege, and opportunity to be called by His name, filled with the Holy Spirit, and adopted into the family of God allows us to look forward to lives and experiences that exceed anything we could have envisioned before accepting and following Christ.

As followers of Christ, we can expect to experience a wide range of emotions and situations, including moments of joy and sorrow and times when we feel overwhelmed, abandoned, or alone. Our journey will include periods of immense strength and confidence alongside many instances of uncertainty, insecurity, and fear. All these experiences are part of the Christian life.

The Christian life is marked by surrender, humility, and sacrifice; it is not for the faint-hearted. Living for Christ is challenging and comes at a significant cost. It requires believing, dedicating, and standing up for what is right. Being a Christian means going against the grain when the rest of the world chooses the easier path. The Christian journey demands a strong commitment and the determination to represent Chris, even when taking the easier route is more appealing. Christians can anticipate periods of feeling isolated, alone, and misunderstood. Every follower of the Lord Jesus is the light in the darkness, life among the dead and dying, and the sweet aroma of righteousness, contrasting with the masses around us who are often engulfed in compromise, wickedness, and depravity.

Christians are called to live distinct and separate lives of service, purpose, and sacrifice. They are ambassadors challenged to remember that when they gave themselves to Christ and received Him as Lord, they ceased to be masters of their destinies, futures, passions, and objectives. On the contrary, they consciously decided to make Christ the Savior and Lord of their lives. The moment Christ is accepted into our hearts, we become legitimate children. The writer affirms this in John 1:13-14 saying, "To all who believed and accepted him, he gave the right to become children of God. They are reborn—not with a physical birth resulting from human passion or plan, but a birth from God." We are no longer our own. We belong to Him entirely.

As followers of Christ, we should expect to be despised, rejected, hated, and opposed. The world often turns against righteousness while embracing wickedness. Since we walk in the light of the Holy Spirit, we can anticipate that the world will reject us, as they reject Him, as we strive to represent and emulate Christ. This should not come as a surprise; Jesus warned us to be prepared for these challenges. In John 15:18-20, Jesus states, "If the world hates you, remember that it hated me first. The world would love you as one of its own if you belonged to it, but you are no longer part of the world. I chose you to come out of the world, so it hates you. Do you remember what I told you? 'A slave is not greater than the master.' Since they persecuted me, naturally, they will persecute you."

The Christian life is not about ease, laziness, and comfort. Instead, it involves surrendering to the Lord, allowing Him to work as He chooses. This journey is often filled with heartache, pain, challenges, and struggles, all for the sake of Christ. Many people mistakenly equate being a Christian with success, wealth, and prosperity. However, faithful followers of Christ prioritize winning souls for the kingdom of God above any temporary or fleeting riches.

The writer admonishes the faithful in Matthew 6:19-21, 24, stating, "Do not store up for yourselves treasures on earth, where moths and vermin destroy, and where thieves break in and steal. But store up for yourselves treasures in heaven, where moths and vermin do not destroy, and where thieves do not break in and steal. For where your treasure is, there your heart will be also... No one can serve two masters. Either you will hate one and love the other, or you will be devoted to the one and despise the other. You cannot serve both God and money." Serving Christ involves sacrifice, self-denial, and living in hope and anticipation of the rewards that await the faithful.

Every genuine Christian can anticipate facing unexpected situations and experiences they could never have imagined. Sometimes, they may encounter attacks, disappointments, and unimaginable losses. It is realistic to expect many relationships to fail, and loved ones, family, and friends may turn away. This is part of the journey and the cost of truly following Christ without compromise. However, Jesus assures us in Matthew 19:29: "Everyone who has given up houses or brothers or sisters or father or mother or children or property for my sake will receive a hundred times as much in return and will inherit eternal life."

While many people embrace the "Christian" title, not everyone is willing to embrace the life and sacrifices required to honor, please, and glorify Christ. Many overlook the words of Christ recorded in Matthew 16:24-26: "If any of you wants to be my follower, you must give up your way, take up your cross, and follow me. If you try to hang on to your life, you will lose it. But if you give up your life for my sake, you will save it. What do you benefit if you gain the whole world but lose your soul? Is anything worth more than your soul?"

As Christians, we should not expect the path to be easy. Jesus never promised that it would be. He reminds us to evaluate, assess, and count the cost. Anyone embarking on this journey must remember that God is not at our service; He has chosen us, granting us the privilege and opportunity to serve Him. He is the Master, and we are expected to be willing servants.

Being a Christian—a follower of Jesus Christ—means committing to His teachings and instructions, which can be challenging and sometimes inconceivably costly. However, we can trust that our God is always faithful and unchanging. He never leaves us alone or without help. He has given us the Holy Spirit, empowering and guiding us to accomplish every good work He has called us to perform.

As Christians, we will encounter suffering in various forms for our faith, and we should view it as a privilege and an honor. The Apostle Paul states in 2 Timothy 2:11-12, "This is a trustworthy saying: If we die with Him, we will also live with Him. If we endure hardship, we will reign with Him." Following Christ requires us to give Him everything. The Christian life demands sacrifice, surrender, tenacity, humility, and the expectation of hardships as the price for faithfully serving our Lord and Master. We should not be alarmed when we face suffering for Christ; if the world hated Him first, we could also anticipate being hated.

The Apostle Peter encourages followers of Christ to embrace the challenges of serving Him. In 1 Peter 4:12-14, 16, he writes: "Dear friends, don't be surprised by the fiery trials you are experiencing, as if something strange were happening to you. Instead, be very glad—these trials make you partners with Christ in His suffering so that you will share in the wonderful joy of seeing His glory when it is revealed to the world. If you are insulted because you bear the name of Christ, you are blessed; the glorious Spirit of God rests upon you... It is no shame to suffer for being a Christian. Praise God for the privilege of being called by His name!"

As Christians, we must recognize that hardship, challenges, and difficulties are inevitable in our service to Christ. However, every believer can rely on God's unwavering presence, who sustains, guides, and leads us. As His children, we find comfort in the assurance that there is no trial or difficulty from which God cannot deliver us. He will always rescue, preserve, and save us because of His love for us and our commitment to Him.

We can expect God's presence and guidance regardless of our trials, challenges, or dangers. He desires to fellowship with us and communicate with us. We are privileged to approach Him in prayer, knowing He hears and responds to our requests. This promise is confirmed in Hebrews 4:14-16, which offers us encouragement with these words: "Since we have a great High Priest who has entered heaven, Jesus the Son of God, let us hold firmly to what we believe. This High Priest understands our weaknesses, for He faced all the same tests we do, yet He did not sin. Therefore, let us come boldly to the throne of our gracious God. There we will receive His mercy and find grace to help us when we need it most."

CHAPTER 16

WHAT IS THE CHRISTIAN LIFE?

Titus 2:7-8, You must be an example to them by doing good deeds of every kind. Let everything you do reflect the integrity and seriousness of your teaching. Let your teaching be so correct that it can't be criticized. Then those who want to argue will be ashamed because they won't have anything bad to say about us."

Christians have a clear directive regarding our behavior and conduct: we must be like Christ. The scriptures tell us that Jesus went everywhere doing good. The good He performed was marked by righteousness and motivated by love for others, along with a desire to help and benefit them. Everything Jesus did honors God, and we are called to do the same in all our actions. As followers of Christ, we are expected to emulate Him. In Antioch, believers were called "Christians" because they resembled Christ closely; they were regarded as "little Christs."

As followers of Christ, we are called to live in peace with everyone. We should love our neighbors as ourselves, treating all people with honor, decency, and respect, especially our fellow believers. The Bible instructs us to value others more than ourselves, prioritizing their affairs, concerns, and needs above our own. We are children of the Great King who cares for and provides for us. Therefore, we are expected to love and care for others just as He cares for them, consistently reflecting His character and love in our actions.

The Bible teaches us that we are called to shine brightly in a dark world and be the salt and light. As a unique people set apart for God's service, He desires us to remain unblemished and undefiled by the pressures and temptations we face, especially since the precious blood of Christ has cleansed us. We are encouraged to be ambassadors for Christ, and if we must endure hardships, let them be for the cause of Christ Jesus rather than because of our actions.

As followers of God, we are encouraged to avoid anything that could bring dishonor or lead to accusations against the cross of Christ. For this reason, Scripture instructs us to "avoid the very appearance of evil." We must ensure that no one can speak ill of our good deeds.

Christians must demonstrate our commitment to following Christ through our behavior. Our conduct should contrast with those who pursue worldly pleasures, often called the "children of darkness," with whom we once identified. In the past, we chased after our desires, indulging in physical cravings and selfish ambitions. The scriptures remind us of the sins we once engaged in, as highlighted in Galatians 5:19-21: "The acts of the sinful nature are obvious: sexual immorality, impurity, debauchery; idolatry and witchcraft; hatred, discord, jealousy, fits of rage, selfish ambition, dissensions, factions; envy; drunkenness, orgies, and the like." As Christians, we must consciously avoid such behaviors and embrace a new way of life.

As children of God, we are chosen to be His representatives and entrusted with the missions given by Christ. The greatest of these missions and commandments is to walk in love. When we walk in love and live in the power of the Holy Spirit, we become trees of righteousness. By keeping our minds focused on God through regular study and meditation on His Word, we are increasingly transformed into His image. When we accepted Christ, we were instantly justified. However, as we continue to walk with Him, the Word of God and His spirit regenerate, renew, and sanctify us daily.

The Bible serves as a spiritual guide for believers, directing our actions, decisions, and motivations. When we are nourished by the Word of God and shaped by Christ, we produce righteous fruits in our lives. Galatians

5:22-25 states: "The fruit of the Spirit is love, joy, peace, patience, kindness, goodness, faithfulness, gentleness, and self-control. Against such things, there is no law. Those who belong to Christ Jesus have crucified the flesh along with its passions and desires. If we live by the Spirit, let us also walk by the Spirit."

As followers and believers in Christ, Scripture reminds us that Jesus has prayed for us, empowering us to fulfill His objectives and desires. In John 17:11, 15-16, Jesus states: "I am no longer in the world, but these are in the world, and I come to You. Holy Father, protect those You have given Me through Your name, so they may be one, as We are. I do not pray that You should take them out of the world but that You should keep them from the evil one. They are not of the world, even as I am not of the world."

Through the power of the Holy Spirit, we are equipped to do God's will, which includes remaining untainted by the world and winning souls for the Kingdom of God.

CHAPTER 17

LOVE IS THE GREATEST GIFT!

Luke 6:35-36, "Love your enemies, do good to them and lend to them without expecting to get anything back. Then your reward will be great, and you will be sons of the Most High because he is kind to the ungrateful and wicked. Be merciful, just as your Father is merciful."

Christians are called to be a light in a dark and troubled world. We have been chosen to represent God's character, nature, and heart to those who feel hopeless. God has entrusted us to be His extensions in this fallen and depraved world. For many people, we may be the only experience of Jesus they ever have. We are expected to act, be, and do as our Savior would. As His ambassadors, ministers, and emissaries, we represent His authentic, genuine, and sincere love.

As followers of Christ, we must embrace the title of "Christian" and strive to reflect His character. Remembering that "Christian" originally meant "little Christ," a name given because His followers resembled Him so closely. Being a Christian requires a deliberate and conscious effort to be like Jesus. This is no easy task; it demands determination, perseverance, and a steadfast commitment to following the guidance of the Holy Spirit.

To be a Christian means adopting the mindset of Christ. As servants of the Lord Jesus, we must be willing to emulate Him by embracing His humility and sacrificial nature. The writer of Philippians 2:5-8 emphasizes this idea: "You must have the same attitude that Christ Jesus had. Though he was God, he did not consider equality with God something to cling to. Instead, he gave up his divine privileges; he took on the humble position of a servant and was born as a human being. When he appeared in human form, he humbled himself in obedience to God and died a criminal's death on the cross."

To be like Christ, we must serve others. As His disciples, followers, and children, we are not above Him; instead, we should be willing to follow and emulate His example of sacrifice and humility. Being a Christian goes beyond merely identifying as one; we are called to demonstrate our faith through words and actions. Most people, without exception, tend to care less about what we know or say until we show how much we genuinely care for them through our actions. We cannot simply claim to love; we must prove it.

The writer reminds us in 1 John 3:16-19, "We know what real love is because Jesus gave up his life for us. So, we should also give up our lives for our brothers and sisters. If someone has enough money to live well and sees a brother or sister in need but shows no compassion—how can God's love be in that person? Dear children, let's not merely say that we love each other; let us show the truth by our actions. Our actions will demonstrate that we belong to the truth, so we will be confident when we stand before God."

As Christians, we are called to be ministers of righteousness, responsible for bringing hope to a fallen and depraved world. Our lives should reflect true goodness, kindness, benevolence, and peace. The world often misunderstands love and has developed distorted notions of it. For this reason, God has chosen us to demonstrate what genuine and authentic love indeed looks like. We are commanded to exemplify God's love, just as Christ did. Scripture supports this by instructing us on how to treat one another as His followers.

1 John 3:23-24 states, "This is his commandment: We must believe in the name of his Son, Jesus Christ, and love one another, just as he commanded us. Those who obey God's commandments remain in

fellowship with him, and he with them. We know he lives in us because the Spirit given lives in us."

God has commanded us to demonstrate love that is "Agape," which means unconditional love. This concept contrasts with the way the world typically understands love. The Greeks had several terms that describe different kinds of love: Eros (romantic and erotic feelings), Phileo (brotherly affection), and Storge (family affection). These terms represent the types of love that many people are familiar with. However, for many, the understanding of love often comes from a self-serving and conditional perspective, reflected in the sentiment, "If you are good and kind to me, then I will be good and kind to you." This attitude limits our depth of understanding and appreciation of love.

Empowered by the Holy Spirit, Christians are called to be examples of true love in a world that often falls short. As followers of Christ Jesus, we are urged and commanded to love unconditionally, without ulterior motives or hidden agendas. We are commanded to love as the Father loves, expecting nothing in return. Loving unconditionally is essential and synonymous to our Father's character and nature; therefore, we must strive to love similarly.

In Matthew 5:43-48, Jesus teaches: "You have heard the law that says, 'Love your neighbor' and hate your enemy. But I say, love your enemies! Pray for those who persecute you. In this way, you will be acting as true children of your Father in heaven, for He gives sunlight to both the evil and the good, and He sends rain on the just and the unjust alike. If you love only those who love you, what reward do you have for that? Even corrupt tax collectors do the same. If you are kind only to your friends, how are you different from anyone else? Even pagans do that. But you are to be perfect, even as your heavenly Father is perfect."

In this context, the Greek word for "perfect," Akribesteron (pronounced ak-ree-bes'-ter-on), refers to doing something more accurately or perfectly. God desires that we love others as perfectly as He loves us. To illustrate this point, the writer states in 1 John 3:16-17: "We know what real love is because Jesus gave up His life for us. Therefore, we should also give up our lives for our brothers and sisters. If someone has enough money to live well but sees a brother or sister in need and shows no compassion, how can God's love be in that person?"

The Apostle Paul, through the Holy Spirit, defines true love in action as Agape—an unconditional and selfless love. This type of love starkly contrasts the world's understanding of love and can only be perfected through Christ. In 1 Corinthians 13:4-7, Paul describes Agape love: "Love is patient, love is kind. It does not envy, it does not boast, it is not proud. It is not rude; it is not self-seeking; it is not easily angered, and it keeps no record of wrongs. Love does not delight in evil but rejoices with the truth. It always protects, always trusts, always hopes, always perseveres."

God desires us to show Agape love to the world, specifically our fellow believers. Through the power of the Holy Spirit, we can accomplish every good work that He has planned for us. Above all, we must exhibit God's grace and love, even in difficult and challenging times. Regardless of our obstacles, we must never forget God's kindness, patience, and generosity toward each of us. This understanding leads us to a commitment, unwavering dedication, and a deep, intimate relationship with the Lord Christ.

The Apostle Paul instructs us on how to live out love and reflect the nature and character of our Father. He reminds us, "Love never fails. But where there are prophecies, they will cease; where there are tongues, they will be stilled; where there is knowledge, it will pass away. We know in part and prophesy in part, but when perfection comes, the imperfect disappears. Now I know in part; then I shall know fully, even as I am fully known. And now these three remain: faith, hope, and love. But the greatest of these is love." As children, followers, emissaries, and ambassadors of the living God, we must love genuinely and authentically!

CHAPTER 18

BENEFITS OF BEING A CHRISTIAN

1 Peter 2:9, "You are a chosen people. You are royal priests, a holy nation, God's very own possession. As a result, you can show others the goodness of God, for he called you out of the darkness into his wonderful light."

What are the benefits of being a Christian? The answer to this question is complex, but there are many advantages to living a Christian life. While being a Christian can be challenging and often lacks comfort or ease, it is not defined by glamour, luxury, fame, or recognition. Instead, it is characterized by sacrifice, discipline, and self-denial. As disciples of the Lord Jesus Christ, we are called to emulate His life and example. We are encouraged to embody Christ-like qualities in our daily lives, actions, interactions, motives, and deeds.

Before becoming a Christian, Jesus advises those who wish to follow Him to consider the cost carefully. He emphasizes that the Christian life should not be taken lightly. While it may not align with the world's standards of desirability, it is the most significant decision one can make for eternal security.

In Matthew 8:19-22, we read: "Then one of the teachers of religious law said to Him, 'Teacher, I will follow you wherever you go.' But Jesus replied, 'Foxes have dens to live in, and birds have nests, but the Son of Man has no place even to lay His head.' Another of His disciples said, 'Lord, first let me return home and bury my father.' But Jesus told him, 'Follow me now. Let the spiritually dead bury their own dead.'

In this passage, Jesus conveys the true essence of following Him. This journey requires sacrifice and self-denial. It does not promise fame, personal glory, or financial rewards. Instead, the Christian life is characterized by humility, modesty, and a commitment to intentionally serving others.

The Christian life is filled with many trials, but God has promised to deliver us from all of them. This promise is explicitly made for believers. As His children, we are heirs to everything He possesses in heaven and earth. We have been completely freed from bondage, slavery, and the penalty of sin. One significant benefit of following Christ is that our names are written in the Lamb's Book of Life, which ensures our eternal security in Him if we hold fast to our faith in Jesus, the author and finisher of our faith.

As followers of the Lord Jesus Christ, we can ask for anything in His name, trusting in faith that it will be granted to us. The Holy Spirit empowers us and carries the authority that raised Jesus from the dead. Our words possess the power of life and death, enabling us to speak things into existence according to God's will and purposes.

As children of God, we are liberated from the power of darkness and the grip of habitual sin. Because we belong to Him, He cleanses and redeems us through His precious blood. We are now called the saints of God, members of a royal priesthood, and part of a holy nation. We are a special people, set apart for God's purposes. As citizens of the heavenly kingdom, we are cherished by God, and each of us is considered God's masterpiece (Poema).

The benefits of being a Christian are both immeasurable and endless. God's promises to those who love Him are infinite. His thoughts about His children are as countless as the sands of the sea and the stars in the sky. However, if I had to highlight one benefit, it would be salvation from sin. The reality that our Savior and Lord Jesus paid the penalty for our sins on the cross at Calvary (Golgotha) nearly two thousand years ago is profound.

The words (tetelestai) "It is finished" represent the greatest blessing that mankind and all of humanity could ever receive.

Benefits of Being a Christian

The benefits of being a Christian are numerous and immeasurable. If we were to list some of these advantages, they would highlight the importance of surrender, obedience, and following Christ.

One significant benefit of becoming a Christian is salvation from the penalty of sin and eternal punishment. This truth is affirmed in John 3:16, which states, "God so loved the world that he gave his one and only Son, that whoever believes in him shall not perish but have eternal life." As Christians, we are no longer enemies of the holy and righteous God. This is emphasized in Romans 5:10-11: "If, while we were God's enemies, we were reconciled to him through the death of his Son, how much more, having been reconciled, shall we be saved through his life! Not only is this so, but we also boast in God through our Lord Jesus Christ, through whom we have now received reconciliation."

As His children, we are transformed from darkness to light, as confirmed in Colossians 1:12-14: "He has qualified you to share in the inheritance of his holy people in the kingdom of light. For he has rescued us from the dominion of darkness and brought us into the kingdom of the Son he loves, in whom we have redemption, the forgiveness of sins."

Furthermore, we are made eternally secure in Christ, as affirmed in Romans 8:35 and 37-39: "Who shall separate us from the love of Christ?... No, in all these things, we are more than conquerors through him who loved us. For I am convinced that neither death nor life, neither angels nor demons, neither the present nor the future, nor any powers, neither height nor depth nor anything else in all creation will be able to separate us from the love of God that is in Christ Jesus our Lord."

As children of God, we are recognized and called His own. According to John 1:12-13, "To all who believed in Him and accepted Him, He gave the right to become children of God. They are reborn—not through a physical birth resulting from human passion or plan, but through a birth from God." We are considered heirs and joint heirs with Christ, the King of Glory, as stated in Romans 8:16-17: "His Spirit joins with our spirit to affirm that we are God's children. And since we are His children, we are His heirs. Together with Christ, we are heirs of God's glory."

We are ambassadors for the living God, the Lord, and Christ. As stated in 2 Corinthians 5:20, "We are Christ's ambassadors; God is making His appeal through us. We speak for Christ when we plead, "Come back to God!" Furthermore, we have the power of the Holy Spirit, as indicated in 1 John 4:13: "God has given us His Spirit as proof that we live in Him and He in us."

As God's children, the Holy Spirit has blessed and empowered us to perform miraculous works, such as casting out demons, healing the sick, and even raising the dead. This is affirmed in Mark 16:17-18: "And these miraculous signs will accompany those who believe: they will cast out demons in My name, speak in new languages, handle snakes safely, and if they drink anything poisonous, it won't harm them. They will lay hands on the sick, and the sick will be healed."

As His children, we have been given the power of prayer, which allows us to communicate openly, actively, and freely with God. This right is reserved for those who belong to Him; He rejects the unbeliever but hears our every request and petition. This is confirmed in Philippians 4:6: "Don't worry about anything; instead, pray for everything. Tell God what you need and thank Him for all He has done. Then, you will experience God's peace, which surpasses all understanding. His peace will guard your hearts and minds as you live in Christ Jesus."

CHAPTER 19

WHAT IS THE CHURCH?

Hebrews 10:25, "Let us not neglect our meeting together, as some people do, but encourage and warn each other, especially now that the day of his coming back again is drawing near."

What is the church? This is an important question, especially for followers of Christ. It is essential to have a clear understanding of the church. Without this understanding, we may be influenced by outside ideas and concepts that do not align with our faith. As people of the Book, the best way to answer the question of what the church is can be found in the Bible, the Word of God. Seeking answers outside of Scripture is not logical. After all, who is better qualified to define His place and worship community than the one being worshipped?

The church is not just a building or structure; it represents something more profound. In the New Testament, the term translated from the Greek word "ekklesia" refers to an assembly, gathering, meeting, or congregation of believers in the Lord Jesus Christ. This concept is familiar to believers, as the Old Testament includes similar expressions, such as "meeting of the Lord" or "the Lord's congregation." The idea of coming together—whether for a gathering, meeting, or assembly—has consistently been recognized as a time for collective and collaborative worship.

Historically, the concept of the church as a specific building, like a tabernacle, temple, or synagogue, was not present in the context of the New Testament. Instead, the term "church," or "ekklesia," has always been understood from a Christian perspective as the assembly, gathering, congregation, and community of followers of Christ—both locally and universally.

The church in the past was quite different from the modern concept we know today. Unlike contemporary churches, which often have a specific appearance and structure, the New Testament church was diverse and varied. The early church was bold, dynamic, and adventurous in its approach. Followers of "The Way" regularly gathered whenever they had the opportunity. Instead of meeting in a designated location, these early believers assembled in various settings, including public spaces, streets, underground areas, synagogues, temples, by the sea, and often in homes, commonly called house churches.

The Church of Christ transcends any building or structure, no matter how elaborate, opulent, or ornate. Physical space does not define it; the church represents believers' assembly, gathering, community, and collective worship. We can understand the true nature of the church by seeking guidance in the scriptures.

In Acts 2:46-47, we read: "They worshiped together at the Temple each day, met in homes for the Lord's Supper, and shared their meals with great joy and generosity— all the while praising God and enjoying the goodwill of all the people. And the Lord added to their fellowship each day those who were being saved." This passage illustrates the essence of the church as a vibrant community of faith.

A building does not define the church; instead, it is the gathering of believers in Christ for worship that constitutes the church. When believers come together—whether in person or virtually—for the specific purpose of collective worship, that is the true essence of the church. Historically, believers would meet daily, and those gatherings were anything but monotonous.

For over two thousand years, the characteristics and practices that define the church of Christ—often referred to as "The Way" or Christians—have remained consistent. These practices include prayer, worship, communal and cooperative prayer, and a focus on mutual spiritual growth and edification. Other essential aspects are fraternal communion, sharing testimonies of Christ's goodness, charity, helping those in need, evangelism, and proclaiming the "gospel"—the good news of Christ—to the world.

The church is the body of Christ, whom He loves and for whom He gave His life. It consists of individuals committed to following "The Way." Jesus stated emphatically, "I am the Way!" In Matthew 28:19, believers are commanded to "Go and make disciples of all nations." Each of us is a part of the church, comprised of individuals, not merely a building or structure. As the Lord's church, we are called to disciple all nations, teaching and instructing people everywhere on how to live in a way that pleases and honors God.

As believers and followers of Christ, we need to remain in fellowship with one another. Coming together allows us to draw strength, encouragement, and support from fellow Christians. The gathering provides opportunities for sharing, learning, and uplifting one another, helping us grow within the safety of our Christian community.

The Bible emphasizes a vital message in Hebrews 10:23-25: "Let us hold firmly to the hope we profess, without wavering, for God is faithful to fulfill His promises. Let us find ways to motivate one another to engage in acts of love and good works. And let us not neglect meeting together, as some are in the habit of doing. Instead, let us encourage one another, especially as the day of His return approaches."

We are not meant to be isolated in our reading, interpretation, study, or fellowship. Instead, we are encouraged to gather frequently as a community of true believers and followers of the Lord Jesus Christ, just as the Church has done for over two thousand years.

The size, color, wealth, or grandeur of a church building does not matter most. What truly matters is that the church is centered around Christ, doctrinally sound, and committed to teaching the Word of God—the Bible. Above all, when choosing a place of worship, the community, congregation, and assembly must prioritize sound, accurate, and uncompromised preaching and teaching of the Scriptures.

When selecting a community or group of believers to join for worship, praying and asking the Lord for guidance in finding a place to feel safe and encouraged to grow is essential. We should seek a community of fellow believers that consistently challenges us to deepen our knowledge and understanding of God's Word. Additionally, it should encourage us to engage in local and community ministry and motivate us to develop and cultivate our talents and gifts as we mature in Christ.

God desires a relationship with us, wanting all of us to grow in our knowledge and love for Him and His beloved Son, Jesus Christ. This growth and development can only happen through an increased understanding, application, and dependence on His Word, the Bible.

Regular and consistent fellowship is essential. Some people believe they can practice their faith alone and in isolation, justifying it with the idea that God is everywhere. However, this perspective is misguided. God designed His church to be a communal, collaborative, and relational experience. Christ Himself instructed us to gather with other believers regularly. God uses our time together and moments of fellowship to speak to, encourage, teach, guide, and inspire us through one another.

CHAPTER 20

CAN MEN AND WOMEN PREACH?

Judges 4:4-5, "Deborah, the wife of Lappidoth, was a prophet judging Israel at that time. She would sit under the Palm of Deborah, between Ramah and Bethel in the hill country of Ephraim, and the Israelites would go to her for judgment."

M any believe the Scriptures oppose women in leadership roles and preaching. However, the passages in 1 Timothy 2:12 and 1 Timothy 3:1-2 are often misinterpreted and do not necessarily reflect a prohibition against women in these roles.

Titus 1:7-9 states that a church leader must be a steward of God's household, living a blameless life without arrogance, quick temper, or dishonesty. He should be hospitable, love what is good, and lead a disciplined life. A strong belief in the trustworthy message he has been taught enables him to encourage others with sound teaching and refute opposition. Additionally, Titus 2:3-5 instructs older women to teach younger women and others. These passages attributed to the Apostle Paul can often be misinterpreted and misunderstood.

While some statements may appear to restrict women's roles as leaders and preachers, this viewpoint is widely challenged and debated across various denominations. Women have been active in all facets of ministry since the very beginning. For example, a woman was the first to witness the risen Savior and to proclaim the good news to her male counterparts. Additionally, many women in the first century served as preachers, teachers, and leaders of house churches long before the development of organized religion, traditions, church governance, and denominations.

The belief that women cannot perform roles equal to men is based mainly on a few phrases attributed to the Apostle Paul. Whether rightly placed or not, these statements must be understood within their historical, contextual, and cultural circumstances. No other writer or apostle addressed women's roles in the church similarly. Paul's letters were directed at specific issues relevant to individual churches, highlighting the unique context of his comments.

The Apostle Paul's words were not meant to be strict commands or lasting restrictions. He lacked insight into the future, the gospel's widespread impact, or the evolution of society. Paul could not have imagined the world expanding beyond his experience. He would likely not recognize today's society, which offers equal access to education, information, rights, and opportunities.

Although these words are attributed to Paul, he spoke to people and churches in different times and cultures, with social practices and traditions that differ from today's. His messages were tied to the specific situations of his context, not timeless principles.

It is unreasonable to conclude that the apostle Paul prohibits women from preaching or holding leadership roles in the church. God is not concerned with gender or titles; He values His servants' work. In 1 Corinthians 3:4-9, Paul emphasizes this by stating that neither he nor Apollos should be elevated above the other, as they are God's servants. What truly matters is the growth that God brings through their efforts. The focus should be on the task rather than who is performing it, as their contributions are essential and will be rewarded.

Women preachers and leaders are valuable servants of God, just like Paul and Apollos. God shows no favoritism and is eager to use anyone willing to serve Him. The belief that women cannot be called to preach or lead in the Church is misguided. Scripture offers many examples of women whom God has empowered for His work.

Leadership has traditionally been perceived as a male role; however, this perception has not always been accurate. Throughout various societies and cultures, women have held authoritative and leadership roles equal to those of their male counterparts. The first female preacher and leader in the Old Testament is the Prophetess Deborah, known for her wisdom and ability to lead Israel to victory. Other notable female preachers include Miriam, Huldah, Anna, and Priscilla.

God uses those He chooses. In the time of the Apostle Paul, traditions and social norms were limiting factors. However, God revealed something extraordinary through the prophet Joel, who spoke of His plans eight hundred years before Pentecost. In Joel 2:28-29, the Lord declares, "I will pour out my Spirit upon all people. Your sons and daughters will prophesy; your old men will dream dreams, and your young men will see visions." God promised to generously give His Spirit to both men and women in the last days, initiating something new that had never been seen before.

On the day of Pentecost, significant miracles occurred as Jews and non-Jews experienced the outpouring of the Holy Spirit, marking a profound shift. Unlike before, when the spirit empowered only a few for limited tasks, many received His indwelling during this event. The Apostle Peter clarified misunderstandings in Acts 2:17-18, quoting the prophet Joel: "In the last days, God says, I will pour out my Spirit on all people. Your sons and daughters will prophesy, young men will see visions, and old men will dream dreams. Even on my servants, both men and women, I will pour out my Spirit, and they will prophesy."

God loves all equally and desires everyone to come to faith in Christ Jesus, regardless of gender. The prophet Joel revealed that God extends His gift to all, irrespective of background or ethnicity. This is affirmed in Acts 10:44-45: "As Peter spoke, the Holy Spirit fell upon all who were listening. The Jewish believers with Peter were amazed that the Holy Spirit had also been given to the Gentiles."

We are living in the last days, and God is doing something new by using both men and women to fulfill His plans for the church. He empowers women in ministry with the same gifts as men and equips those He has chosen. The truth is clear: God has poured His Spirit on women just as He has on men. Despite opposition, the success of countless ministries led by women demonstrates this. While it may not align with traditional ideals, God uses any means necessary to fulfill His purposes.

We must humbly acknowledge that none of us truly understands God's mind. His thoughts and ways are different from and higher than our own. The Scriptures provide clear examples of God acting according to His will, even when it contradicts logic, reason, or human understanding. In Numbers 22, God uses a donkey to fulfill His purpose. According to Numbers 22:28, "The Lord gave the donkey the ability to speak." The donkey was allowed to challenge his master Balaam's actions, asking, "What have I done to you that deserves you beating me three times?" If God could use a beast of burden, nothing impedes His ability to use a woman in any manner He chooses.

The traditional leadership model has predominantly featured men. However, that is not the complete picture. Throughout history, God has also used women as leaders. Women have historically held leadership roles in the church. The position and belief that they are restricted and cannot be leaders is modern. Women have always been crucial to the church and are not inferior to men when they have the same abilities. In the New Testament, neither men nor women were specifically called pastors, but both engaged in pastoral functions like teaching and caring for others. The Apostle Paul mentions several women in ministry roles, including Phoebe, Prisca, Mary, Junia, Tryphena, Tryphosa, and Persis, in Romans 16:1-6.

There is a strong and compelling case for both male and female leaders and pastors. God can and will use whomever He desires. Despite misinterpretations of the Apostle Paul's statements, God continues to empower women in ministry and church leadership. We must remember his affirmation in Galatians 3:28: "There is neither Jew nor Gentile, neither slave nor free, nor male and female, for you are all one in Christ Jesus. Since you belong to Christ, you are true heirs of Abraham and his promises."

Regardless of differing opinions on female leadership in the church, it's crucial to understand that these views are human constructs, not God's intentions. God does not favor one gender over another; He calls everyone to bear fruit and fulfill their work. Evidence shows that God is moving in a new direction, answering the prayers of the faithful by sending women to serve as laborers in His mission field, especially as the harvest is plentiful and the laborers are few. Despite resistance, God has kept His promise. The presence of women preachers, teachers, pastors, and leaders fulfills Joel 2:28-29, which says, "I will pour out my Spirit on all people. Your sons and daughters will prophesy... Even on my servants, both men and women, I will pour out my Spirit in those days."

CHAPTER 21

WHAT IS THE BIBLE?

---

2 Timothy 4:3-4, "The time will come when men will not put up with sound doctrine. Instead, they will gather many teachers around them to suit their desires to say what their itching ears want. They will turn their ears away from the truth and turn aside to myths."

Many new believers and non-believers ask, "What is the Bible?" The answer is quite simple: the Bible is the Word of God, given to holy men through the inspiration of the Holy Spirit and recorded for future generations. The term "Bible" comes from the word "Biblios," which means "book." However, the Bible is not just a single book; it is a collection of several books written over a long period by different authors from diverse backgrounds and geographical locations. No other collection or compilation is quite like it. Unlike other texts that may make similar claims, the Bible that Christians refer to is undeniably the inspired and breathed Word of God—Jehovah, the God of Israel and the world.

The Protestant Bible

The Protestant Bible, the Canon, comprises sixty-six books divided into the Old and New Testaments. The Old Testament contains 39 books, ranging from Genesis to Malachi, while the New Testament has 27 books, from Matthew to Revelation. Throughout the Bible, the spirit of God works through human authors to convey and reveal His mind, character, plan, will, and love for creation. From beginning to end, the Old and New Testaments tell an incredible love story, culminating in the sacrificial death of the Lord's Christ, Jesus, the Son of God.

The Catholic Bible

The Catholic Bible differs only slightly from the Protestant Canon. While the Catholic Bible includes all the books in the Protestant Bible, it also has several additional books known as the Apocrypha or Deuterocanonical books. The Catholic Bible contains a total of 73 books. These extra books are Tobit, Judith, Wisdom (the Wisdom of Solomon), Sirach (also called Ecclesiasticus), Baruch, 1 Maccabees, and 2 Maccabees. Although these books were historically esteemed and respected, Jewish tradition did not recognize them as scripture.

Understanding how the Bible has been passed down to us as Christians can be a lengthy and complex process. However, the most straightforward and direct response regarding the scriptures is that they are the word of God. They can transform lives, free lost men and women, and save dying souls. In 2 Timothy 3:16-17, the writer expresses this idea by stating, "God inspires all Scripture. It is useful for teaching us what is true and helping us recognize what is wrong in our lives. It corrects us when we are wrong and instructs us on how to do what is right. God uses it to prepare and equip His people to do every good work."

For believers and followers of Christ, the biblical scriptures are our most cherished treasure. There is no more remarkable asset than the word of God, which holds immense significance for us. Nothing in this world can compare to it. For Christians, the word of God is a source of life; it guides, leads, directs, and instructs us while also providing comfort to the brokenhearted and uplifting the weary soul.

The psalmist emphasizes the significance of God's word in Psalm 119:9-16: "How can a young person stay pure? By obeying your word. I have tried hard to find you; don't let me wander from your commands. I have hidden your word so I might not sin against you. I praise you, O Lord; teach me your decrees. I have recited aloud all the regulations you have given us. I rejoice in your laws as much as in riches. I will study your commandments and reflect on your ways. I will delight in your decrees and not forget your word."

The word of God nourishes and sustains the believer's soul, connecting us to Christ and allowing Him to communicate with us during moments of silence, quiet reflection, and meditation. Through His word, God guides us, reveals Himself, and deepens our knowledge, wisdom, and understanding of the truth. We learn to recognize His voice, mind, heart, will, power, and love through His word, offering us insight into God's incomprehensible nature. This truth is expressed in Hebrews 4:12-13: "The word of God is alive and powerful. It is sharper than the sharpest two-edged sword, cutting between soul and spirit, between joint and marrow. It exposes our innermost thoughts and desires. Nothing in all creation is hidden from God. Everything is naked and exposed before His eyes, and He is the one to whom we are accountable."

Unlike many other books that fade in popularity over time, the Bible has remained a bestseller for centuries. It has consistently changed and transformed the lives of countless millions of readers. The Bible's impact on humanity is broader than any other book written. Its influence is so profound that individuals with evil intentions have attempted to destroy and erase it from existence throughout history. Nevertheless, millions have willingly risked and sacrificed their lives to preserve it. Many men and women have suffered and died for their confidence, devotion, and faith in the life-changing words contained within its pages. As a result, the Bible continues to endure.

The Bible is not only inspired; it is the "Logos," the breathed words of God to humanity. It is the only book that has proven infallible, accurate, specific, and detailed regarding past, present, and future historical events. Written by forty-two authors over a span of 1,600 years, it is intricately woven together to suggest that only God Himself could be the actual author, using willing individuals as conduits to convey His message to mankind.

As the word of God, the Bible is all that followers of Christ need to succeed in every area of life, provided they believe in its teachings and apply them practically. The scriptures offer clear and definitive instructions to guide us on our journey. Inspired by the one who knows all things—past, present, and future—the scriptures address life's most challenging questions and provide practical solutions. The Bible is our most incredible resource for instruction, guidance, direction, and teaching on living surrendered lives consecrated, set apart, and wholly committed to serving our Savior, Lord, and God.

Knowing Jesus without the Bible is impossible, as He is called "The Word" made flesh. The Bible contains truths about Him from beginning to end. Christ Himself instructs us to "learn of me," the only way to do this is by spending time in the Bible, God's Word. Jesus affirmed this reality when He rebuked the religious leaders of His time, saying in John 5:39-40, 46: "You search the Scriptures because you think they give you eternal life. But the Scriptures point to me! Yet you refuse to come to me to receive this life... If you believed Moses, you would believe me because he wrote about me."

For Christians, the Bible is as essential as water is to a fish; it is neither a luxury nor an option. It is vital for living and growing in spiritual maturity and knowledge of Christ. The Bible nourishes the soul and enriches life because it is alive—it is the living Word. The writer of Hebrews 4 affirms, "The word of God is living and powerful, and sharper than any two-edged sword, piercing even to the dividing asunder of soul and spirit, and of the joints and marrow, and is a discerner of the thoughts and intents of the heart." In the words of French Emperor Napoleon Bonaparte, "The Bible is no mere book, but a Living Creature, with a power that conquers all that oppose it."

CHAPTER 22

WHAT IS PRAYER?

Mark 14:38-39, "Keep alert and pray. Otherwise, temptation will overpower you. For though the spirit is willing enough, the body is weak. 39 Then Jesus left them again and prayed, repeating his pleadings."

What is prayer? It is one of the most important aspects of a believer's life. For Christians, prayer holds the utmost significance, closely followed by the daily reading and study of biblical scriptures. It serves as the foundation of the Christian experience and is essential for both success and spiritual growth. Without prayer, believers may struggle to understand and experience God's guidance. Just as air is vital for the body, prayer is critical for the Christian spirit.

Prayer allows us to connect with God, communicate with Him, express our love, and share our requests. It is a dialogue in which we can voice our concerns and listen to His guidance. God, desiring to have a relationship with us, provided a way to commune with Him without barriers. Regularly, He seeks to share and reveal aspects of His intentions and plans for our lives. God wants to spend time with us and unveil the plans He has for us. We can find answers to our most pressing questions through prayer and patiently waiting in His presence.

Prayer is Christians' most potent weapon against our adversaries' schemes and plans. It is essential for the life of every believer. Ephesians

6:12 reminds us, "We do not wrestle against flesh and blood, but against the rulers, against the authorities, against the cosmic powers over this present darkness, and the spiritual forces of evil in the heavenly places." Since our struggle is against these spiritual forces, God has given us a crucial tool: prayer.

Prayer holds a vital place in the life of a believer. One of its essential functions is cultivating a deeper intimacy with our Savior and nurturing our relationship with God. We learn to listen for and rely on God's voice for direction and guidance through prayer. It also helps us develop strength and spiritual resilience. When we encounter overwhelming situations, we can present our concerns, worries, anxieties, and fears to God in prayer. This practice helps us understand that God is always present, and even in moments of silence, He is teaching us to trust Him. During these silent times, we realize that His timing is intentional. We learn that even when He seems to delay, He responds and answers every petition made in prayer.

Prayer is a unique and powerful aspect of believers' lives, possessing the undeniable ability to create change and transformation. It promotes inner peace, breaks personal, spiritual, and mental strongholds, and fosters emotional and mental healing. Moreover, prayer initiates forgiveness and reconciliation, cultivates gratitude, and enhances perseverance and patience. It also provides guidance for important life decisions. Through prayer, believers experience growth and maturity, strengthening their faith and deepening their spiritual understanding and development.

As followers of Christ, we are reminded that our struggle is not against other humans but against spiritual adversaries. 2 Corinthians 10:3-4 says, "We are human, but we don't wage war as humans do. We use God's mighty weapons, not worldly weapons, to knock down the strongholds of human reasoning and to destroy false arguments." Since prayer is not a worldly action, it is a powerful tool we can use anytime and anywhere. Prayer cannot be restricted, bound, or hindered. Even if we whisper our requests during the darkest night or amid a violent storm, our prayers will reach the attentive and waiting ear of our great and awesome God.

Prayer should always be our first response in every situation. It is a powerful tool available to us. Through prayer, we can influence the course and outcome of any circumstance because we invite God into the scenario. Where God is present, limitless possibilities exist, and His presence generates immediate change. Involving God in our decisions is always the best decision we can make, as He deeply cares for the welfare of His children. As stated in Jeremiah 29:11, "I know the plans I have for you," says the Lord. "They are plans for good and not for disaster, to give you a future and a hope."

Sometimes, we may feel that God isn't listening. However, this is far from the truth. God is always present and attentive. No matter our circumstances, we can be assured that God hears us whenever we call out to Him. He never sleeps nor slumbers. The writer assures us in Exodus 22:23: "If you afflict them in any way, and they cry out to Me, I will surely hear their cry." Even when His response is not what we desire, we must understand that His delay is not necessarily a denial. We can be confident that whatever He does is in our best interest.

The scriptures encourage us to pray continually. In 1 Thessalonians 5:16-17, we are reminded, "Rejoice always; pray without ceasing." This passage highlights the importance of maintaining a spirit of prayer and keeping our hearts open to petition and thanksgiving before the Lord, our God. Through prayer, we should consistently bring our requests to God on behalf of ourselves and others, trusting that every outcome works for our good. The scriptures teach us that through prayer, we must knock and keep knocking on the doors of heaven, confident that God's will and perfect plan will answer our requests.

Through prayer, we can bring our cares and concerns to God. This practice teaches us to trust Him and to wait patiently for His responses to our requests. Prayer allows us to develop a closer and more intimate relationship with the Lord. As followers of Christ, engaging in this form of worship helps us experience a more fulfilling, enriched, and empowered life. Prayer allows us to lay down every burden and fear, knowing that God is more than willing and able to bear and carry them with His love.

CHAPTER 23

WHAT IS THE HOLY SPIRIT?

Luke 11:11-13, "You fathers—if your children ask for a fish, do you give them a snake instead? Or do you give them a scorpion if they ask for an egg? Of course not! So, if you sinful people know how to give good gifts to your children, how much more will your heavenly Father give the Holy Spirit to those who ask him."

The Holy Spirit represents God's essence, power, and tangible presence. Commonly referred to as the "Spirit" or the Holy Ghost, the Holy Spirit is not an impersonal force; instead, He is a personal being, equal to the Father and the Son. The Holy Spirit embodies God's very character and is recognized as the third person of the Trinity. Scripture describes His characteristics: He is intelligent (1 Corinthians 2:10-11), possesses emotions (Ephesians 4:30), has a will (1 Corinthians 2:11), commands (Acts 8:29), teaches (John 14:26), and intercedes on behalf of believers in prayer (Romans 8:26).

While some may not adhere to the doctrine of the Trinity—the belief in one God existing in three distinct persons—the Bible explicitly supports this teaching. As stated in 1 John 5:7, "There are three that bear record in heaven, the Father, the Word, and the Holy Ghost: and these three are one."

Various names know the Holy Spirit, but He is consistently recognized for His purpose, authority, and power. Throughout Jesus' ministry on earth, it was through the power of the Holy Spirit that the blind received their sight, the lame were able to walk, the demon-possessed were freed from their torment, the sick were healed, and the dead were brought back to life. Additionally, it is by the power of the Holy Spirit that God created the worlds and the universe. The Holy Spirit is the active and dynamic essence and power of God.

Without the active presence of the Holy Spirit in a believer's life, it is impossible to lead effective and victorious lives in Christ. Through the power of the Holy Spirit, we can walk in the newness of life and fulfill God's commandments. Without the Spirit, we cannot overcome the traps and snares of the world. The Holy Spirit assists us in resisting temptations, desires, and longings that go against righteousness. Without His guidance, we are like ships without sails, tossed about aimlessly with no defense or direction. The Holy Spirit provides the power, direction, and power necessary to please God.

In the life of a believer, the power and presence of the Holy Spirit are essential. He helps, directs, guides, comforts, and empowers Christians. Acknowledging the importance of this supernatural power, Jesus told His disciples in John 14:15-17, 26, as He prepared to return to the Father: "I will ask the Father, and he will give you another Advocate who will never leave you. He is the Holy Spirit who leads you into all truth. The world cannot receive him because it isn't looking for him and doesn't recognize him. But you know him because he lives with you (now) and will be (in) you later. No, I will not abandon you as orphans—I will come to you... "When the Father sends the Advocate as my representative—that is, the Holy Spirit—he will teach you everything and remind you of everything I have told you."

Every Christian needs the power of the Holy Spirit in their life. The Holy Spirit empowers us to live according to the calling that God has placed on us as His followers. Only through the Holy Spirit can we overcome our old, sinful nature that once dominated our lives. Without the Holy Spirit working within us, we would remain enslaved to our flesh's ambitions, passions, motives, and desires. Additionally, without the Holy Spirit, we have no chance of standing against our adversary, Satan, who is both crafty and subtle. The Bible warns us about our enemy in 1 Peter 5:8: "Be sober, be vigilant; because your adversary the devil, as a roaring lion, walks about, seeking whom he may devour."

Jesus shared with His disciples the power of God available to them through the Holy Spirit, saying, "You will do even greater works than I do." The Holy Spirit is the divine force that ensures the renewal of the body and the soul. Without the Holy Spirit's power in a Christian's life, we are prone to repeated defeats and face immense spiritual battles, leading to overwhelming frustration and disappointment. In contrast, the Holy Spirit empowers, strengthens, and encourages us to build and advance the kingdom of God and the body of Christ.

The Holy Spirit grants believers spiritual gifts to advance His church. Equipping believers for divine service, the writer of Ephesians 4:11-12 states, "He gave some to be apostles, some to be prophets, some to be evangelists, and some to be pastors and teachers, for the perfecting of the saints, for the work of the ministry, for the edifying of the body of Christ."

The scriptures affirm that those who win souls for the Kingdom of God are wise. The Holy Spirit empowers believers with the boldness to be spokespersons and ambassadors for Christ. On the Day of Pentecost, when the power of God descended upon the believers, the writer notes in Acts 4:31, "When they had prayed, the place where they were assembled was shaken; and they were all filled with the Holy Spirit and spoke the word of God with boldness."

Through the Holy Spirit, we become what God desires us to be. The Holy Spirit enables us to walk in God's strength, renewing our minds, hearts, and desires. Because of the work of the Holy Spirit in our lives, we seek to fulfill God's will and yield to His guidance. We can be transformed into God's image and likeness through the Holy Spirit's power.

As the Holy Spirit works within us, we gradually become trees of righteousness, bearing fruit pleasing to God. In Galatians 5:18-25, the scriptures contrast the works of the flesh with the fruits of the Spirit: "When the Spirit leads you, you are not bound by the law of Moses. Suppose you follow the desires of your sinful nature. In that case, the results are evident: sexual immorality, impurity, lustful pleasures, idolatry, sorcery, hostility, quarreling, jealousy, outbursts of anger, selfish ambition, division, envy, drunkenness, wild parties, and other sins like these. I warn you again, as I have before that anyone living this kind of life will not inherit the Kingdom of God.

The Holy Spirit produces this fruit: love, joy, peace, patience, kindness, goodness, faithfulness, gentleness, and self-control. There is no law against these qualities! Those who belong to Christ Jesus have nailed their sinful passions and desires to His cross and crucified them there. Since we live by the Spirit, let us follow the Spirit's leading in every aspect of our lives."

CHAPTER 24

WHAT ABOUT SPEAKING IN TONGUES?

---

1 Corinthians 14:5, "I would like every one of you to speak in tongues, but I would rather have you prophesy. He who prophesies is greater than one who speaks in tongues unless he interprets so that the church may be edified."

What is speaking in tongues? Tongues are one of the spiritual gifts given to believers in the early church as signs, evidence, and demonstration of the power and presence of the Holy Spirit in the believer's life. Tongues were a clear and indisputable sign and proof of the believer's salvation and acceptance of the Lord Jesus Christ, regardless of cultural or ethnic background.

From a biblical perspective, speaking in tongues is one of the many gifts of the Holy Spirit available to believers in Christ Jesus. While tongues can be mimicked, they cannot be taught; the ability to speak in tongues is a gift from God that He bestows upon whomever He desires. Historically, the capacity to communicate in an unlearned or heavenly language was widely recognized as a miraculous gift from God. Although the gift of tongues has not ceased, there are instances today where misunderstandings, apprehensions, and even abuses of this remarkable and sometimes flashy gift occur.

According to scripture, the first demonstration of this gift occurred on the day of Pentecost when believers gathered in a specific place, united in prayer and agreement. Acts 2:1-4 states: "On the day of Pentecost, all the believers were meeting together in one place. Suddenly, there was a sound from heaven, like the roaring of a mighty windstorm, filling the house where they were sitting. Then, what looked like flames or tongues of fire appeared and settled on each of them. And everyone present was filled with the Holy Spirit and began speaking in other languages, as the Holy Spirit gave them this ability."

On the day of Pentecost, the remarkable manifestation of this gift occurred in two significant ways. First, it fulfilled the promise made by Jesus about the evidence of his faithful followers and believers in him as the Christ. In Mark 16:17, Jesus states, "These signs will accompany those who believe: In my name, they will drive out demons; they will speak in new tongues." Second, this manifestation served to honor, praise, glorify, and worship God for His great and marvelous works, as reflected in Acts 2:11: "Both Jews and converts to Judaism, Cretans, and Arabs—we hear them declaring the wonders of God in our own tongues!"

Although often misunderstood, miraculous gifts manifest in the personal prayer time of spirit-filled believers. At times, we may feel unclear or unaware of how to pray, and in those moments, the Holy Spirit intercedes for us, praying through us in tongues or in a language that is unknown to us. Sometimes, while praying in tongues, the Holy Spirit explores the deeper desires—the faithful meditations of our hearts and minds—and brings our petitions before God. Humans often pray amiss, asking for things we should not. However, through prayer in our heavenly languages and tongues, the Holy Spirit communicates directly with the Father, addressing matters we may be unaware of or in the way they should.

Like all gifts, speaking in tongues is meant to edify and strengthen the church or assembly of believers. It was never intended for amusement, entertainment, or display. The apostle Paul states in 1 Corinthians 14:2, "Anyone who speaks in a tongue does not speak to men but to God. Indeed, no one understands him; he utters mysteries with his spirit." Unfortunately, misunderstandings about the purpose of this remarkable gift often led to its misuse, particularly within the church. As a result, many people develop apprehensions about this gift and may even assert that it, along with other gifts, has ceased to operate and function in the lives of modern-day believers.

When the gift of tongues is misused in a church assembly, it can create significant confusion for those who are uneducated, unfamiliar with church practices, or not accustomed to these types of spiritual gifts. Contrary to the beliefs of some, the gift of tongues is alive and active across various cultures, ethnicities, and denominations. It is undeniable that the gift of tongues has not ceased among believers. However, this miraculous gift's differing purposes, intentions, and applications in various traditions have led to profound misunderstandings, abuses, and confusion.

There should always be a desire for order in the Lord's house, as God is not the author of confusion. Clarity and understanding regarding the gift of tongues are essential. The Scriptures offer clear and definitive guidelines on tongues' proper use and purpose when believers gather. While these instructions are not absolute, they provide a reasonable and practical model for establishing order, particularly within the early church.

All spiritual gifts are given to believers in Christ for personal and collective edification. In 1 Corinthians 14:2-5, the apostle Paul states, "If you speak in tongues, you are talking only to God, since people won't understand you. You will speak by the power of the Spirit, but it will all be a mystery. However, the one who prophesies strengthens, encourages, and comforts others. A person who speaks in tongues is strengthened personally, but one who speaks a word of prophecy strengthens the entire church. I wish you could all speak in tongues, but even more, I wish you could all prophesy. Prophecy is greater than speaking in tongues unless someone interprets what you are saying so that the whole church will be strengthened."

In this passage, the Apostle Paul highlights the significance of prophecy over speaking in tongues in communal settings of believers. This distinction is critical unless someone has the gift of interpretation, which allows the entire assembly to be spiritually edified and built up. Contrary to some beliefs, tongues have not ceased nor require them or God's gift of tongues. Countless men and women worldwide continue to operate in this gift, regardless of their tradition, ethnicity, or cultural background. God graciously pours out His Spirit and still uses all spiritual gifts.

There is a common misunderstanding in some church denominations that speaking in tongues is necessary to prove the Holy Spirit's active presence in a believer's life. In these denominations, a believer's salvation may be questioned or considered invalid if they have not received the gift of the Holy Spirit, evidenced by speaking in tongues. However, this belief is inaccurate and unsupported by scripture. The gift of tongues is not required to confirm a believer's genuine conversion. Scripture indicates that the Holy Spirit distributes various gifts to believers, not just tongues.

To address this misunderstanding among the believers in the church in Corinth, the Apostle Paul stated in 1 Corinthians 12, "Dear brothers and sisters, regarding your question about the special abilities the Spirit gives us, I don't want you to misunderstand this. There are different kinds of spiritual gifts, but the same Spirit is the source of them all. A spiritual gift is given to each of us so we can help each other. To one person, the Spirit gives the ability to give wise advice; to another, the same Spirit gives a message of special knowledge. The same Spirit gives great faith to another, and the one Spirit gives the gift of healing to someone else. He gives one person the power to perform miracles and another the ability to prophesy. He allows someone else to discern whether a message is from the Spirit of God or another spirit. Still, another person can speak in unknown languages, while another is given the ability to interpret what is being said."

The gift of tongues is terrific. However, it is not the only or most important gift. No gift is exceptionally superior to another. All gifts among believers work collaboratively to build and perfect the body of Christ, His universal church. There is too much emphasis and importance on the gift tongues, perhaps because it is one of the most flashy and identifiable gifts. However, this should not be. The apostle was in no way against the gift of speaking in tongues. On the contrary, in 1 Corinthians 14:18, he said, "I thank God that I speak in tongues more than any of you. But I would rather speak five understandable words to help others in a church meeting than ten thousand words in an unknown language."

Each spiritual gift is designed to bring enrichment, encouragement, edification, and growth. God, the giver of all gifts, is the one who determines which gifts believers will receive. While all believers are filled with the same Holy Spirit, they do not all receive the same gifts.

To explain how God distributes spiritual gifts among humanity, the Apostle Paul states in 1 Corinthians 12:27-31, "You are the body of Christ, and each of you is a part of it. In the church, God has appointed first apostles, second prophets, third teachers, then workers of miracles, those with gifts of healing, those who can help others, those with gifts of administration, and those who speak in different kinds of tongues. Are all apostles? Are all prophets? Are all teachers? Do all work miracles? Do all have gifts of healing? Do all speak in tongues? Do all interpret? But eagerly desire the greater gifts."

An overemphasis on the gift of tongues often pressures individuals to imitate those who have genuinely received this specific gift. While speaking in tongues is indeed a unique and miraculous gift that all should desire, the gift that is ultimately more beneficial for the assembly of believers is the gift of prophecy and interpretation.

The apostle Paul highlights this in 1 Corinthians 14:4-5 saying, "A person who speaks in tongues is strengthened personally, but one who speaks a word of prophecy strengthens the entire church. I wish you could all speak in tongues, but even more, I wish you could all prophesy. For prophecy is greater than speaking in tongues, unless someone interprets what you are saying so that the whole church will be strengthened."

The gift of tongues is a remarkable spiritual gift but not the most important one. No spiritual gift is superior to another. According to Scripture, the gift of tongues serves several identifiable purposes in a believer's life.

One key purpose of speaking in tongues is as a sign for unbelievers. The manifestation of tongues, as seen on the Day of Pentecost, demonstrates God's power and presence in believers' lives. Additionally, tongues can provide individual and personal spiritual edification. This private aspect of speaking in tongues allows believers to experience a deeper and more intimate connection with the Savior.

The Apostle Paul supports this view in 1 Corinthians 14:2, stating, "If you can speak in tongues, you will be talking only to God, since people won't be able to understand you. You will speak by the power of the Spirit, but it will all be mysterious." Furthermore, speaking in tongues is a powerful demonstration of the Holy Spirit's work in the believer's life.

The primary purpose of the gift of speaking in tongues is to build up and edify the church community, strengthening the assembly of believers. Every gift that God bestows upon believers through His immeasurable grace is intended to uplift, build, and perfect His church, and the gift of tongues is no exception. The apostle Paul emphasized that while tongues are miraculous gifts, they are not superior to others.

In 1 Corinthians 14:12-17, Paul states, "Since you are so eager to have the special abilities the Spirit gives, seek those that will strengthen the whole church. Anyone who speaks in tongues should also pray for the ability to interpret what has been said. If I pray in tongues, my spirit is praying, but I don't understand what I am saying. So, what should I do? I will pray in the Spirit, and I will also pray in words I understand. I will sing in the Spirit, and I will also sing in words I understand. If you praise God only in the Spirit, how can those who don't understand you join in praising God with you? How can they give thanks when they don't know what you're saying? You may be giving thanks very well, but it won't strengthen the people who hear you."

CHAPTER 25

WHAT IS BAPTISM?

Mark 1:8, "I baptize you with water, but he
will baptize you with the Holy Spirit!"

What is baptism? Many ideas and opinions surround this practice, but numerous beliefs are incorrect, unfounded, and poorly supported. The methods and significance of baptism vary widely across different denominations. In some reformative traditions, baptism is viewed not as an option but a requirement for salvation. Many denominations place enormous emphasis on the ritual of baptism, considering it one of, if not the most essential and necessary, acts in the lives of followers of Christ.

Baptism is undeniably an important decision and event in the life of a follower of Christ. However, it is both unfounded and unbiblical to equate the ritual of baptism with salvation. While baptism holds significant meaning as a rite and sacrament, it is not a requirement for salvation. Regardless of whether one is baptized, the grace of God and the power of the Holy Spirit are sufficient for salvation, with or without the act of baptism.

While some teach and believe that baptism is necessary for salvation, the scriptures challenge and affirm the opposite view. Those who support the idea that baptism is essential for salvation often cite the Apostle Peter's words in Acts 2:38: "Each of you must repent of your sins and turn to

God and be baptized in the name of Jesus Christ for the forgiveness of your sins. Then you will receive the gift of the Holy Spirit." However, concluding that baptism is a prerequisite for salvation is incorrect and misguided. Salvation comes through faith in Christ alone. No action, ritual, or separate work can add to or enhance the perfect and complete work of atonement and redemption our Lord and Savior accomplished on the cross.

Baptism holds a deep, rich, and profoundly symbolic significance in conveying extraordinary spiritual truths; however, it does not possess any salvific power. The scriptures repeatedly emphasize that we are saved by faith alone. As stated in Ephesians 2:8-9, "God saved you by his grace when you believed. And you can't take credit for this; it is a gift from God. Salvation is not a reward for our good deeds, so none of us can boast about it."

Baptism represents our belief, faith, and connection with Christ Jesus, our Savior and Lord. Although baptism has no power to save, it serves as a public and outward demonstration of our identification with Christ. By participating in the ritual of water baptism through immersion, we make an explicit declaration of the truth and message of salvation. The Apostle Paul says in 1 Corinthians 15:3-4, "I passed on to you what was most important and what had also been passed on to me. Christ died for our sins, just as the Scriptures said. He was buried and raised from the dead on the third day, just as the Scriptures said."

We display our union with Christ through baptism in His death, burial, and resurrection. In Galatians 3:27, the writer emphasizes, "All who have been united with Christ in baptism have put on Christ, like putting on new clothes." While the ritual of baptism holds significant meaning, it is not part of the process of salvation. The Apostle Paul clarifies this in Romans 6:3-4 by stating, "Have you forgotten that when we were joined with Christ Jesus in baptism, we joined Him in His death? For we died and were buried with Christ by baptism. And just as Christ was raised from the dead by the glorious power of the Father, now we also may live new lives."

Water baptism symbolizes being buried with Christ, signifying that we are now dead to the power of sin. Rising from the watery grave represents our new life in Him—our spiritual resurrection and union with Christ. Baptism is a visible sign of the inward grace we have received, declaring that we are no longer slaves to sin but have been made alive in Christ Jesus. It beautifully illustrates renewal, commitment, and belonging to God's family.

Baptism does not save us; we are saved solely through faith in Christ. Salvation is a gift given by God's unmatched grace and is not based on anything we have done or can do. This message is affirmed in Titus 3:4-7: "When God our Savior revealed His kindness and love, He saved us, not because of the righteous things we had done, but because of His mercy. He washed away our sins, giving us a new birth and life through the Holy Spirit. He generously poured the Spirit on us through Jesus Christ, our Savior. Because of His grace, we have been made right in His sight, giving us confidence that we would inherit eternal life." While baptism is not necessary for salvation, it serves as our testimony of the inward assurance we have received when passing from death to life.

When asked about baptism in many churches, people assert that Jesus commanded it, suggesting it is essential for eternal life. However, this interpretation is not entirely accurate. Baptism serves as a rite of initiation into the church. Baptism and conversion are so closely linked in the New Testament that one often implies the other. However, neither is necessarily dependent on the other. We are saved without baptism.

The Formula

Many misunderstandings about baptism exist. There is also much contention about how baptism should be performed, precisely the words used. Some believe that it is imperative that we are baptized in "Jesus" name, or we are still in sin, unsaved, and destined for eternal damnation. Again, this is an inaccurate supposition and unsupported scripturally and historically.

While some may not fully understand or acknowledge this truth, the phrase "in Jesus' name," as recorded in Acts 2:38 and other passages, does not present itself in an explicit or required manner. On the contrary, this phrase emphasizes the authority of Jesus Christ in baptism. It reflects the understanding of the early church followers that the power to perform baptism rests in Christ Jesus, the risen Savior and Lord. This aligns with the declaration made by Jesus in Matthew 28:18, where He stated, "All authority has been given to Me in heaven and on earth."

From the church's earliest days, the Trinitarian formula found in Matthew 28:19 has been widely accepted as the proper method for baptism. Early Christian writings, such as the Didache—a Christian manual from the late first or early second century—instruct believers to baptize "in the name of the Father, and of the Son, and the Holy Spirit." This practice reflects the early church's understanding of Jesus' command in the Great Commission and emphasizes the importance of administering baptism correctly.

It is a common misconception that baptism must be performed "in Jesus' name"; otherwise, it is deemed ineffective, leaving us still in sin and unsaved. A more accurate interpretation is that to baptize in "Jesus' name" means to baptize under the authority of Christ, recognizing His Lordship. This understanding does not contradict the historical Trinitarian formula but harmonizes and complements it. Through the name of Jesus, we access the grace and power of the fullness of the Godhead—Father, Son, and Holy Spirit.

In Matthew 28:19-20, Jesus delivered "The Great Commission," instructing his followers to "Go and make disciples of all nations, baptizing them in the name of the Father, the Son, and the Holy Spirit. Teach these new disciples to obey all the commands I have given you." In this passage, Jesus highlights the importance of bringing individuals into the church, a process closely linked to baptism. This connection explains why the doctrines of baptism and the Church of Jesus Christ are so closely intertwined.

Before the coming of Christ, baptism was a significant step for converts entering the Jewish faith, and people in the New Testament era were quite familiar with this practice. The Bible mentions in John 1:19 that when priests and Levites confronted John the Baptist, they did not ask, "What are you doing?" but rather, "Why do you baptize?"

Before the early Christian church was established, it was common for an outsider who wished to embrace Judaism to undergo a process of instruction in the faith. This included circumcision, followed by a period of healing, after which the individual would immerse themselves in water during a ceremony witnessed by others. The presence of witnesses was crucial in this process. This was typical for individuals to be accepted into the church or synagogue. After immersion, the individual would receive all the rights and privileges associated with Judaism.

Christianity began as a Jewish sect, and many often forget this vital point. The process for a Gentile (a non-Jew) to become a part of the Christian community followed a similar procedure to that of Jewish converts. However, circumcision was no longer a requirement. Acts 15:18-20 states, The Lord has spoken—He who made these things known so long ago.' So, I believe we should not make it difficult for the Gentiles to turn to God. Instead, we should write and tell them to abstain from eating food offered to idols, from sexual immorality, from eating the meat of strangled animals, and from consuming blood." This change eliminated distinctions between men and women, clarifying that Christianity breaks down traditional barriers during initiation into the faith.

Baptism is the rite of initiation into the Christian community. Like its Jewish predecessor, baptism must be voluntary and witnessed. It should be administered after a confession of faith, as outlined in Romans 10:9-13, "If you openly declare that Jesus is Lord and believe in your heart that God raised him from the dead, you will be saved, for it is by believing in your heart that you are made right with God and by openly declaring your faith that you are saved. As the Scriptures tell us, "Anyone who trusts in him will never be disgraced." Jews and Gentiles are the same in this respect. They have the same Lord, who gives generously to all who call on him. "Everyone who calls on the name of the Lord will be saved."

The Lord Jesus entrusted His church with two necessary sacraments: Communion and Baptism. Both sacraments should be observed and cherished by followers of "The Way," those who follow the Lord Christ.

Concerning Communion, also known as the Eucharist or the Lord's Supper, the Apostle Paul writes in 1 Corinthians 11:23-26, "I pass on to you what I received from the Lord himself. On the night he was betrayed, the Lord Jesus took some bread and thanked God for it. Then he broke it into pieces and said, "This is my body, which is given for you. Do this in remembrance of me." In the same way, he took the cup of wine after supper, saying, "This cup is the new covenant between God and his people—an agreement confirmed with my blood. Do this in remembrance of me as often as you drink it." Every time you eat this bread and drink this cup; you announce the Lord's death until he comes again." Regarding baptism, the apostle says in Romans 6:4, "We were therefore buried with him through baptism into his death."

In Romans 6, the Apostle Paul explains that baptism allows believers to participate in Christ's death, which lays the groundwork for their future resurrection and ultimately leads to eternal life. However, Paul does not imply that a person who converts on their deathbed and dies before being baptized would be excluded from salvation. The idea that baptism is a requirement for salvation contradicts Scripture.

If baptism were a prerequisite for salvation, we would face a significant challenge in interpreting the event that occurred after the Apostle Peter preached the gospel to a Gentile (non-Jew) in Acts 10. The scripture states, "Even as Peter was saying these things, the Holy Spirit fell upon all listening to the message. The Jewish believers who came with Peter were amazed that the gift of the Holy Spirit had also been poured out on the Gentiles. They heard them speaking in other tongues and praising God. Then Peter asked, 'Can anyone object to their baptism, now that they have received the Holy Spirit just as we did?' So, he ordered them to be baptized in the name of Jesus Christ."

Cornelius and everyone in his household who heard and accepted Christ were immediately saved. They received the gift of the Holy Spirit, evidenced by their speaking in unknown tongues before they were baptized. Thus, baptism does not save; instead, it serves as a public demonstration of our inward grace and a ritual rite of acceptance into the Church, signifying our alignment, association, and identification with Christ.

CHAPTER 26

WHAT IS COMMUNION?

Luke 22:19-20, "He took some bread and thanked God for it. Then he broke it in pieces and gave it to the disciples, saying, "This is my body, which is given for you. Do this in remembrance of me." After supper, he took another cup of wine and said, "This cup is the new covenant between God and his people—an agreement confirmed with my blood, which is poured out as a sacrifice for you."

What is Communion? Known or called by several names, Communion is one of the two sacraments given to His church by the Lord Jesus Christ.

Communion, also known as the Eucharist, Holy Communion, or the Lord's Supper, is a sacred act that fosters fellowship with God and among believers. It is a moment when followers of Christ remember His unparalleled sacrifice on the cross at Calvary. The Lord Jesus instituted communion for His followers and disciples to commemorate His death and sacrifice. Communion serves as a proclamation, remembrance, and celebration of Christ's atoning death. During this celebration, believers partake of bread and wine, although wine is substituted with grape juice in many traditions.

The elements used to represent the body and blood of Christ are bread and wine. Only wine and no other liquid should be used (Matthew 26:26-

29). Believers "feed" on Christ's body and blood, not through physical means, but rather through the soul and by faith, which is considered the mouth or hand of the soul. This spiritual feeding occurs through the power of the Holy Spirit. Importantly, this "feeding" on Christ happens during the Lord's Supper and whenever faith in Him is exercised.

The Last Supper

Just before Judas Iscariot betrayed Jesus in the Garden of Gethsemane, Jesus gathered His disciples in an upper room to celebrate the Passover. It soon became apparent that there was an additional purpose for their gathering. Matthew 26:26–29 says, "While they were eating, Jesus took bread, and when he had given thanks, he broke it and gave it to his disciples, saying, 'Take and eat; this is my body.' Then he took a cup, and when he had given thanks, he gave it to them, saying, 'Drink from it, all of you. This is my blood of the covenant, which is poured out for many for the forgiveness of sins. I tell you, I will not drink from this fruit of the vine until I drink it new with you in my Father's kingdom."

The concept of this ordinance is referenced in various passages throughout the scriptures, including Matthew 26:26-29, Mark 14:22-25, Luke 22:19-20, and 1 Corinthians 11:24-26. Communion serves several essential purposes. Specifically, it is meant to commemorate the death of the Lord Jesus Christ. Additionally, it acts as a sign and seal, applying the benefits of the new covenant to every believer. Through this ordinance, the Lord Christ affirms His promises to His chosen and elected followers, who, in turn, solemnly dedicate themselves to Him and His service. Furthermore, communion promotes the fellowship of believers in Christ Jesus, symbolizes the mutual connection among believers, and serves as a badge of the Christian faith for all believers.

Early Church Communion

After the death, resurrection, and ascension of Jesus, the early church followed His teachings and practiced the ordinance of communion—this involved eating bread, which symbolizes His body, and drinking wine, which represents His blood. The apostle Paul emphasized the concept of fellowship during communion by stating, "Is not the cup of thanksgiving for which we give thanks a participation in the blood of Christ? And is not the bread that we break a participation in the body of Christ? Because there is one loaf, we are many, are one body, for we all share the one loaf" (1 Corinthians 10:16–17). Communion not only fulfills Jesus' commandment but also fosters unity among believers.

The Apostle Paul also warned those who might approach communion carelessly or disrespectfully: "Whenever you eat this bread and drink this cup, you proclaim the Lord's death until he comes. Therefore, whoever eats the bread or drinks the cup of the Lord in an unworthy manner will be guilty of sinning against the body and blood of the Lord. Everyone should examine themselves before eating the bread and drinking from the cup. For those who eat and drink without recognizing the body of Christ eat and drink judgment upon themselves" (1 Corinthians 11:26–29).

Communion allows believers to express their love for and connection with Christ publicly. It serves as a remembrance of the atoning sacrifice that Jesus made for humanity and lets us look forward to the time when He will share in fellowship with us in His kingdom.

CHAPTER 27

WHAT ABOUT TITHING?

Luke 6: 38, "Give, and you will receive. Your gift will return to you in full, pressed down, shaken together to make room for more, running over, and poured into your lap. The amount you give will determine the amount you get back."

What does the Bible say about tithing? What is it, and what does it mean? These are excellent questions that deserve a clear and straightforward response.

Tithing refers to the practice of giving, specifically the giving of ten percent of one's income or resources. This practice was established so that the people of God could return a portion of what they received to the Lord, who gave them all they had. In the Old Testament, specifically in Leviticus 27:30, it states, "One-tenth of the produce of the land, whether grain from the fields or fruit from the trees, belongs to the Lord and must be set apart to Him as holy."

The significance of tithing in ancient Israel is quite different from its interpretation today. In the past, tithes were an essential aspect of worship and a means of maintaining a relationship with Yahweh, the God of Israel. Since the people were primarily agricultural, God commanded that one-tenth of their produce and livestock be set aside. For the Israelites, the tithe represented the understanding that everything belonged to God. It was not merely a transactional act but a covenantal acknowledgment of God's immeasurable generosity and ownership. Tithing served to express gratitude and reliance on God's ongoing provision.

One memorable example of giving the tithe is the Old Testament narrative between the patriarch Abraham and Melchizedek. The scripture states in Genesis 14:18-20: "Melchizedek, the king of Salem and a priest of God Most High, brought Abram some bread and wine. Melchizedek blessed Abram with this: 'Blessed be Abram by God Most High, Creator of heaven and earth. And blessed be God Most High, who has defeated your enemies for you.' Then Abram gave Melchizedek a tenth of all his recovered goods."

The misunderstanding and overemphasis on tithing in many churches today have made it a significant issue and a point of contention. As a result, many people refuse to participate or abandon the biblical exhortation to offer a portion of their resources to the Lord. Due to the misrepresentation of tithing by many churches, individuals are denied the opportunity to engage in this essential communal and individual worship as they might otherwise wish.

In the Old Testament, tithing was a requirement of the Law. However, many churches overlook that Israel was obligated to offer several tithes due to a lack of understanding and misinterpretations regarding its meaning, significance, and purpose. This is indicated in Leviticus 27:30, Numbers 18:26, Deuteronomy 14:24, and 2 Chronicles 31:5.

Upon closer examination of the original intent behind the multiple tithes—one designated for the Levites, one for the use of the temple and feasts, and one for the poor—it becomes clear that the total amount contributed would have reached around 23.3 percent. Many scholars now understand tithing in the Old Testament as a form of taxation meant to provide for the needs of the priests and Levites within the sacrificial system.

The Law of Moses was given to the people of Israel, and as Gentiles and non-Jews, we have never been subject to such a law. While the Law had specific demands, Christ Jesus fulfilled its requirements through His death. Nowhere in the New Testament is there a command, suggestion, or demand for Christians to adhere to the legalistic tithing system.

We are no longer under the law; instead, we are members of the New Testament church.

The emphasis that many churches place on tithing is misinformed and misguided. The passage used in most churches to support giving is Malachai 3:9-10, "You are under a curse, for your whole nation has been cheating me. Bring all the tithes into the storehouse for enough food in my Temple. "If you do," says the Lord of Heaven's Armies, "I will open the windows of heaven for you. I will pour out a great blessing; you won't have enough room to take it in! Try it! Put me to the test!"

So often, this passage in Malachai is taken grossly out of context. This has nothing to do with the New Testament church or believers. In the book of Malachai, Israel was charged with the offense of robbing God. They had proven themselves faithless, violating and breaking their covenant. Repeatedly, they turned away from their God, as He consistently pleads for their return. It was for that reason that they were cursed. Israel had grown distant and cold, moving ever further away from their God, which had once been their first love. Israel began robbing God by bringing only a portion of their obligation to the temple. In their tight-fisted, self-centered state, they were cheating God by failing to bring Him the whole tithe and the required offerings to the temple. They were taking what belonged to God and using it for themselves. So, God called and challenged the people to return to Him and receive a great blessing they could not contain.

As New Testament believers, we are not bound by the Old Testament law and are not required to give a mandatory tithe as the people of Israel were. Instead, we can voluntarily and willingly provide a portion of God's blessing. God encourages us to contribute to the church so that important ministry work can continue. This includes preaching, teaching, evangelism, missions, feeding the hungry, clothing the needy, and addressing the needs of the less fortunate. He desires that our giving comes from the heart—willingly, enthusiastically, and cheerfully. God loves a cheerful giver and wants us to recognize that everything we have comes from Him.

The New Testament does not explicitly command us to tithe. However,

God deserves nothing less than our best regarding time, attention, obedience, devotion, and resources. He consistently provides for us and demonstrates immeasurable love and kindness. We owe everything to the Lord. Our willingness to show that He owns our lives through generous, cheerful giving is the least we can do. When we are stingy with our time and resources, keeping it primarily for ourselves, and neglect to pray, worship, and serve others, we, like Israel, are essentially robbing God.

While the New Testament does not require Christians to tithe, it emphasizes the importance and benefits of giving. As followers of Christ, we are encouraged to give according to our abilities. Sometimes, we feel led to give more than ten percent, and others when we may provide less. Our contributions should reflect our capacity and the needs of the body of Christ.

Every Christian should regularly pray and seek the Lord's guidance, as suggested in James 1:5: "If you need wisdom, ask our generous God, and he will give it to you. He will not rebuke you for asking." God loves a cheerful giver. Our giving and offerings should always come from pure intentions and motives, stemming from a heart of service and worship.

In 2 Corinthians 9:7, we are reminded: "You must each decide in your heart how much to give. And don't give reluctantly or in response to pressure, for God loves a person who gives cheerfully."

THE NICENE CREED

We believe in one God,
the Father almighty,
maker of heaven and earth,
of all things visible and invisible.
And in one Lord Jesus Christ,
the only Son of God,
begotten from the Father before all ages,
God from God,
Light from Light,
true God from true God,
begotten, not made;
of the same essence as the Father.
Through him, all things were made.
For us and for our salvation
he came down from heaven;
he became incarnate by the Holy Spirit and the Virgin Mary,
and was made human.
He was crucified for us under Pontius Pilate;
he suffered and was buried.
On the third day, he rose again, according to the Scriptures.

He ascended to heaven
and is seated at the right hand of the Father.
He will come again with glory
to judge the living and the dead.
His kingdom will never end.
And we believe in the Holy Spirit,
The Lord, the giver of life.
He proceeds from the Father and the Son,
And with the Father and the Son is worshiped and glorified.
He spoke through the prophets.
We believe in one holy catholic and apostolic church.
We affirm one baptism for the forgiveness of sins.
We look forward to the resurrection of the dead,
And to life in the world to come. Amen.

THE APOSTLES CREED

I believe in God, the Father almighty,
Creator of heaven and earth.
I believe in Jesus Christ, his only Son, our Lord,
Who was conceived by the Holy Spirit
And born of the virgin Mary.
He suffered under Pontius Pilate,
was crucified, died, and was buried;
He descended to hell.
The third day he rose again from the dead.
He ascended to heaven
and is seated at the right hand of God the Father almighty.
From there, he will come to judge the living and the dead.
I believe in the Holy Spirit,
the holy catholic* church,
the communion of saints,
the forgiveness of sins,
the resurrection of the body,
And the life everlasting. Amen.

www.ingramcontent.com/pod-product-compliance
Lightning Source LLC
LaVergne TN
LVHW041323080426
835513LV00008B/575